D1596694

The Struggle To Be Human

THE STRUGGLE TO BE HUMAN

Crime, Criminology, and Anarchism

Larry Tifft
and
Dennis Sullivan

Cienfuegos Press

The Struggle To Be Human: Crime, Criminology, and Anarchism
by Larry L. Tifft and Dennis Sullivan
© Published 1980 by Cienfuegos Press, Over The Water, Sanday, Orkney,
KW17 2BL, U.K.

British Library Cataloguing in Publication Data

Tifft, Larry L
  The struggle to be human.
  1. Law
  I. Title II. Sullivan, Dennis
  340   K355

  ISBN 0–904564–31–2
  ISBN 0–904564–30–4 Pbk

Photoset, Printed and bound by
REDWOOD BURN LIMITED
Trowbridge & Esher

Contents

Publisher's Foreword

Statist criminology treats of illegal crime, which is the least of society's serious problems and is treated as the greatest. The existence of illegal crime is presented as an apologia for the state on the supposition that it can only be thwarted by a governmental machine. The existence of legal crime is seldom admitted or, if occasionally so, as, for instance, in the undeniable criminality of Hitler's regime doubts are cast by statists on the legality of such a regime. For this reason the Nazi leaders were "tried" in a "court of law" for acts undoubtedly legalized by the German state, on the entirely mythical supposition of a higher legal authority, which boils down in the finish to the fact of their having lost the war in which they engaged. There can be little doubt that the Russian leaders could equally have had their crimes against humanity exposed and were in fact only accepted as "legal" and "beyond outside interference" because their armed forces happened to be the stronger – in other words, because they retained the power of the state.

The origins of the state, or the rise of any ruling class, however it may curb itself with democratic or constitutional restraints, are no different from that of any oligarchy of crime; the Mafia, had it only existed longer or dug its roots deeper, would be not a government of crime but a government of law, though in that event its operations, though legalized, would both be of greater criminality and have greater scope for criminality.

The worst of illegal crimes to the state is treason and subversion, against which the harshest penalties are exacted. Yet if successful they prove not to be illegal at all, and if sufficiently successful not even so to those who are betrayed or subverted. Benedict Arnold is regarded as a traitor though he stood by the constitutional and legal government; who would ever apply the epithet to the rebel George Washington? Within twenty years of his death the most bigoted British Tory had ceased to do so, so established in "law" had the once revolutionary American State become! But Guy Fawkes is annually given a derisive celebration as a traitor.

The state, established by force and maintained by repression – to whatever degree that is required for its safe existence – determines what is *legal*. A dictatorial state will legalize genocide, even of its own population, and it is fatuous to suppose there is anything "illegal" about this. It might be that illegal methods are employed for a party advocating such a program to win power, but once it does so all its actions are "legal". Resistance becomes illegal crime and – except in cases of war, and then only when it suits the other side – is regarded as banditry. But can such resistance be regarded as delinquency or a crime against society? On the contrary, it is the highest virtue.

It is fashionable today to talk of "violence" rather than of "crime" but the same logic persists. What is denounced by the media, that is, resistance to the state, is "illegal violence". What is extolled and extenuated is legal violence. When one reads in the press that "terrorists have sabotaged a nuclear rocket base" the debasement of language can go no further.

The recent history of Spain provides an illuminating example. When the generals rose in rebellion against the very state and motherland to which their own conception of duty lay, soley because they did not like the way things were going, this was stigmatized as a crime by the Spanish government but by no other since it was done by an army having the magic of "legal authority" and not by a disorganized rabble within the armed forces. The army rapidly made itself a government and the situation was regularized internationally by suggesting there were two de facto governments – one constitutional, one military – and the prize of being the de jure government to go to whichever won the civil war. It was not regarded as illegal, however, or even "violent" or "terrorist", to take one side or the other. With the victory of Franco, many would not accept this fact; but as the world war rapidly ensued, this was not universally condemned. Britain had an interest in encouraging resistance forces in Nazi occupied Europe and including Spain. It refrained from attacking them, on occasions it used them. The same resistance using the same methods went on, certainly as far as the anarchists were concerned, for a whole generation afterwards; but after 1945 it became "criminal", "terrorist" and, biggest metamorphosis of all, "violent" and so diffused was the cant that resistance had somehow become anti-social, because "violent", that it spilled over into the very libertarian ranks themselves.

The greatest problem facing the world today is the enormous powers now available to the state and disposed of by the establishment. Besides these powers of death, destruction and despoliation every other problem falls into insignificance. But this form of legal crime, even though we have seen how readily it can be committed by those who will use any means, illegal or legal, to obtain control of the state for crimes against society as such, receives minor attention, attention that is dismissed as cranky; it is the "anti-flouride belt" that is concerned with such matters. But with every backing of the popular media, the entire population, of all levels of understanding, can be raised into frenzy about a few kids who go out on a Saturday night snatching handbags. In England it is safe to walk the streets at all hours and so low is the rate of crimes against the person that such crimes naturally occupy greater public attention than in countries where they are the norm. It is quite correct that crimes against the person should be treated with horror; but this horror is expressed in a steady and insidious campaign, which goes down to the grass roots, to increase the strength of the repressive machinery of the state which is the biggest criminal of all and which is the least to be trusted. There is thought to be no greater argument against a stateless society than the one which demands our wallets should be protected, against the depredations of individual villains, by the very state that preys on those wallets. And the suggestion that a proportion of the young muggers might have skin of a different colour or come from a different cultural background from those of the majority is enough to justify, in a disturbingly large number of minds, the claims of the most criminal of statists.

In reality this problem is minor – but we must not toss it aside for all that. A libertarian criminology should be prepared to answer the problems of crimes against society, differentiating them clearly from crimes *against* the state, which are often no crimes at all, or the crimes *by* the state against society which are overwhelming and form the anarchist case against statism.

No anarchist could be a criminal against society. One may say this with dogmatic certainty for automatically a person guilty of rape, antisocial murder, exploitation, governmentalism, or the imposing of external authority by force upon another could no more be an anarchist than a vegetarian can be a person who eats pork chops, roast beef or stewed mutton. The question is not whether a person understands this or that ideology or acknowledges this or that organization but whether they are what they profess to be, and the divisions between authoritarian and libertarian are nowhere more clearly seen than in crime.

An anarchist is, very often, stigmatized as a criminal by the state, or may enter into activity hostile to the interests of the state. Anarchist philosophy is by its nature the enemy of the state. It therefore is quite possible that the anarchist may enter into illegal activities but never into antisocial ones.

Is burglary, for instance, antisocial? The property laws treat all forms of burglary with like severity; but there is antisocial burglary and illegal burglary (not to mention legal burglary which is the worst of all). The speculator or dishonest financier who robs people of their savings, whether legally or illegally – and the dividing line is very fine in practice – is antisocial. But could one say, however, that the burglar who robs banks or tax offices or bookmakers is antisocial? Not to glamourize such people (they are not necessarily Robin Hoods either), but they are not posing any threat to society – that is to say, to people living in tranquillity.

Going back to the gangs of kids who, realizing an organized few can always defeat a mass of unconnected individuals, are undoubtedly taking a cheap and easy way out of their immediate poverty and are a pest to society: they have taken their cue from the law of bourgeois society which says "Enrich yourself"; they have been incited by the glamourous advertisements showing the rewards to which they can aspire; they are petty authoritarians showing their strength (collective) against weakness (individual). If they were to become libertarians they would not be lifting wallets, except in the National Sporting Club, and their muggings would be against the military machine.

But there is a big difference as to how the media, and ultimately the police and the courts, would treat them. They would no longer be a non-political pest against which the remedy would be a highly politicized police force. On the contrary: they would be a "menace to society," a "dangerous criminal conspiracy" to overthrow the fundamentals of living together. It does not matter in the least now whether criminals are socialists or conservatives or liberals or fascists; indeed the majority tend towards right wing or centre extremism and are therefore socially acceptable – unless they belong to a racial minority, when they become a "national menace." If they were libertarians then not only would they be major criminals, but the whole libertarian movement would be deemed responsible, not only internationally, but for all time – even if they were only held to be anarchists by their actions and did not so profess themselves. Yet the effect on the public would have been to reduce their actions to a mere affair of business operations and the elimination of personal violence or the element of exploitation.

"Society" – which is to say the whole process of living together – becomes jeopardized on the issue of personal violence, one person against another. It is patent that one cannot condemn all violence and regard on a par the defensive forms of violence with the aggressive. Was it "murder" that Maria Spridinova was guilty of when she shot down the Tsarist general guilty of innumerable anti-social murders? – and insisted on taking the responsibility? Is she to be condemned as a "terrorist" and he exalted as a "victim of terrorism"? This is an extension of the statist ideology which says we not only may but should kill, rape and loot for the state but never resist that evil which the state says is lawful, a handy doctrine for judges.

What then should be our source of moral guidance? It used to be the church, the servant of the state. Often the church was perverted into a defence of the state whatever it did. (Murder was no murder when it was lawful killing and the bishops blessed the banners of the warriors.) Often enough the bishops taught a morality of their own little better than the moral chaos they were supposed to be combatting. But at any rate at one time people were restrained by a notional ethic that characterized some actions as *bad* and some as morally indefensible. The notional ethic was anchored to an empty superstition in which no one now believes. There are therefore no restraints to which one can reasonably point – what is a frail or elderly woman to say to deter a thug encountered on a lonely path? That God is watching him? The best outcome of that would be he might regard her as a harmless old eccentric.

Community is the only real moral force and always has been. The belief in solidarity, in mutual aid, in guaranteed freedom, which is the only guarantee of a tranquil society, is rooted in anarchism, and the state deprecates and even suppresses such notions.

With the lack of moral sanctions against crimes against society comes the demand for increased legal sanctions, which do not deter in the least. Does reliance on the police work? Pick up the newspapers of any modern capital and you can see it does not. The strengthening of the police force can put down subversion but it cannot deal with crime because it is too vast. They can smash a printing press, they cannot patrol every lonely highway and byway. And the stronger and more effective the police force may be, the weaker and less organized is the public which demands protection. For the state to be all, the people must be nothing; for the police to be effective in dealing with crime the people must be rendered ineffective. The police invite co-operation; certainly they want individuals as informers, as auxiliaries. But if the people are strong enough to deal with anti-social measures, the police are nothing. Imagine a workers' patrol able to deal with local offenses of exploitation and oppression, able to suppress rapists, and capable of dealing with break-ins – and imagine it being acceptable in a statist society!

Having put the problems of delinquency in its proper place, it still remains to be dealt with. It has not occupied a great space in anarchist theory, Peter Kropotkin brushing it aside contemptuously. In a free society there will be no crime. Crimes against property will go when the concept of property goes. Any critique of deviance and criminology from a libertarian point of view will owe, nevertheless, a great deal to Kropotkin and, more recently, to Alex Comfort, who has pioneered its study.

For though criminology is a minor concern of society as a whole, against the crimes of the statists, it is of major importance as the last defence of statism. Thus criminology must be rescued as a discipline from the statists and one needs to see how the problems of criminal delinquency arise and how it can be treated. Unless a convincing anarchist criminology can show that without an institutionalized police force and without the inhuman invention of the prison system it will be possible for society to live peacefully, people will turn to the criminal state – reluctantly – but still dependent on it, still hoping that by democratic reform they may somehow decriminalize it.

The authors have produced an important libertarian analysis of the issues of justice, crime, punishment and freedom, and although primarily concerned with raising questions of social, criminal, statist and medical injustice in the United States the analysis is applicable worldwide and we hope the questions raised here will provide our readers with food for thought, discussion and, most important of all – action!

STUART CHRISTIE

SOLIDARITY TO ALL AND THANK YOU/All who have struggled/Pa – for love, direction and care; Pat (Beerbelly and Bones) – Waiting for the right audience/Stuart, Albert – for joining our struggle to share this/John, Larry, and Bernie – for support and aid/Chicago – despair but for Gerald, J.B., Duff, Carl, LaMar, Pat L., Sroka, Scully, Jim and Betty, Murry/Dan Glaser – humane teacher/Hugs, reality and companionship – Love, Brandy, Quin/Joffre – there will always be others to lift the message/No words-partner-Cook – there was nothing good enough so I alone came/Bob and Sandy, Phipps, Ken, Mer – though this may be, Thursday nights just aren't the same/Parentage from the gentle and moral/ Michigan – Joyce, Nina, John, Scott, Rod, Marie, Arlene, Richard, Gill and Jim J. – especially the songs/Visits, protection, 48 hours of Joe Hill and all your worries – thanks Ma/John and Michael – the way it should be/Picnics and fellowship – unitarians/Discussions and friendship – Cardell and Bill/Pat, Hans, Jim, Sandy, Sid – support within the factory/Nanny – may there always be fire on the mountain/ Hal – it was important not to be alone/and thank you D./ Parentage – Ellis Island/Joseph – lived and died fifty years too soon, knowing/Gloria – never flinching from the dark once/Patricia – who has done what we say/Kimmy – beginning her journey young/Erin – I would save you/Beau – touching the center of earth/Baobab Community – all brave and grown with big love roots/Allen Goldberg – Albert Schweitzer is alive and well in Troy/George Fischer – still a flower/Michael – we will share the women, we will share the wine/Sharon – Assisi and Michael – angel/Jim Coyne, Tony Sculley – all the saints of Grand St./Casey – tougher odds than most/Leslie T. – more than Cambridge chair, a theatre full/John Ferguson – open hearth/Scott – one load already given/Mary D. – never quitting/Bob S., Tom D. – life line in New York State factory/Mark Guthridge – Whitman's ghost/ Jack Miller – Newburgh's final sunflower/T. – animae dimidium meae.

                              The man
Of virtuous soul commands not, nor obeys.
Power, like a desolating pestilence
Pollutes whatever it touches, and obedience,
Bane of all genius, virtue, freedom, truth,
Makes slaves of men, and, of the human frame,
A mechanized automaton. ·

                                                    Shelley

Introduction: The Struggle To Be Human

Modern criminology is on the brink of extinction. It is now beyond the possibility of further evolution. It has evolved to the point where it can no longer contain the contradictions it has bred for its own survival and the survival of the state. Dinosaurs of method, criminologists have eaten their way out of a world of values, hollowed out of any conscience. The strange irony is that criminologists, as all social scientists, having made their way and survived by claiming themselves to be neutral and value-free, are now faced with value decisions that are personally staggering. They must now choose either to be subsumed into an energy force of the impending fascism of the nascent police state in America or to transform themselves into scientific energies that foster discovery of how persons can balance their human and spiritual needs with the natural rhythms of the universe. The present choice cannot be made as choices once could, with the tedious arguments of scientific rationalism and detachment, but only through personal statement and presence. Like Whitman, each of us must come forth to proclaim: "I and mine do not convince by arguments: we convince by presence."

Though we have flourished in the academic tradition of liberal or state criminology, we no longer find any credibility in the theories and ideas we have inherited from our ancestors. In large part, this book dramatizes the bartering of our professional birthright for personal meaning and quality of life. We no longer see any possibility of quality of life for anyone within the present capitalist economic order or in any related party dictatorship arrangements. (We use "party dictatorship" to refer to the party controlled state economic

1

arrangements commonly designated "state socialist" or "communist state." Such designations are often references to current U.S.S.R., Cuba, and the People's Republic of China. "Socialist state" is a non sequitur, a contradiction which, by associating socialism with the concept of state, denigrates the meaning of socialism.) We see criminology as a major propaganda force that serves to mask the deadening force of the present system of economics and any real possibility for human community. For centuries criminologists have sung folk tales about the wrong wars. They have promised peace with weapons of destruction. While the state ushers humanity down the path of destruction, criminologists continue to serve up their tidy ideological diversions and masks for the economic and state elites.

We believe that why people hurt each other cannot be reduced to rational cause-and-effect relationships that exclude the struggle for economic and social equality, methodologies that reduce human experience to the narrow confines of "problem." We believe that punishment and forgiveness cannot realistically have meaning through sterilization and psychosurgery, brutal methods of caging, beatings and the persistent isolation of persons from sound, light and human touch. We believe that the questions of harm are related to the human struggle for "a cosmic sense" and are linked to the belief that we must travel far if we are to find reasons for a man overpowering a woman in the shadows of American parks and kitchens. We believe that, without a distant journey that incorporates community and restores primacy to the human and natural, we will continue to transform ourselves into nonhuman forms of life. The human person suffers acutely from "a nostalgia for which there is no remedy upon earth except as is to be found in the enlightenment of the spirit – some ability to have a perceptive rather than an exploitative relationship with his fellow creatures."[1]

The dramatization toward a collective consciousness is begun. There is an outright refusal on the part of the criminologists and other social scientists to pledge allegiance to state definitions of crime, punishment and institutional arrangements which both constrain thinking about the injustices of the world and the potential for beginning community and foster the belief that social injustices are unrelated. We cannot speak of the machine-gunned bodies at Attica without in the same breath talking about the falling bodies of starving people in East Asia, the burning bodies of Vietnamese children, the rain-leaking ceilings of the houses in Troy, New York, the function and nature of the abstract power of the state and capitalism. To begin to deal with the state is to begin to deal with the others.

That social, political and personal justice, equality and freedom are possible within the megatechnics of corporate capitalism and its gigantic web of spreading multinationals, the state and its network of institutions is grand illusion. That it is possible to utter the words "criminal justice" and intend not to give credence to economic and social justice is also illusion. And thoughts about economic and social justice are wasteful flights of fantasy unless the state is given the opportunity to die once and for all and primacy given to human experience as the only meaningful source of human authority. As Diane Wakowski says: "Justice is reason enough for anything ugly. It balances the beauty in the world."

As Copernicus could find meaning in the orbits of the planets only if he looked at their movement from the sun, not the earth, and lifted himself imaginarily from the earth to put himself on the sun,[2] so we propose that we can never find meaning or freedom in living if we consider life processes from the floundering orbits of law, the state or corporate economy, but only through lifting ourselves to the warmth of experience and human community. We have sacrificed enough life at the self-centered altar of centralization and war machine. We now know that its appetite for the consumption of human life is endless.

At the same time, we recognize that the possibility exists that we may never be capable of life without god or state, but it is first imperative that we risk their eternal loss until we get a firm grasp on our humanity and experience the freeing authority of human experience. Until we have done so, we

3

must continue to reject forms of authority that are external to human experience and relationship, that tie the human soul in estranging knots. How willing we are to assume such a frame of mind, how willing we are to allow the bloody icons of law and the state to drift into oblivion will determine how we will respond to the meaning in this book and our own lives. For some the end of the book begins here.

If what we address as criminology does not sound familiar, it is because we no longer are familiar. We no longer think or act the same. No longer can we sit squat on the weighty methodological mushrooms of certainty, puffing on the numbing hookah of calculation and control. We believe that what people think and feel about the world is very much tied to how they feel and think about themselves. Thinking about the world and the development of social theory cannot take place outside the experience of the theorist, much less without it. If criminologists are to reflect the life concerns of the world, they themselves must become part of the organic processes of the world and its struggles. If we are concerned about the natural rhythms of the world, we must at the same time be engaged in the search for our own natural rhythms.

There are two facets to the same process of experience – the transcending of the atomized self and our own personal fears, and the transcending of social theories which do not speak to economic and social injustice, to the human condition, to human misery, to human potentiality, to community. We must confront the conflagrations and destruction set off by militarism and an economy based on military destruction and the warmaking of nation states while at the same time confronting the conflagrations of our personal belief systems, traditional lifestyles and values. We are not really concerned about hunger unless we eat differently, about peace unless we act differently, about human relationship unless we begin to deal with ageism, sexism, and the crass forms of racism and classism in our own lives.

But without involvement in a community of concern, no worthwhile social theory is likely to develop. Without personal statements about integrating our own lives in community

4

issued in the form of social theory, the worthwhile actions of many persons are likely to be fragmented and reduced to frantic, isolated attempts to counteract or eradicate hierarchical relationships. Without social theory which seeks at all costs the primacy of human experience and at the same time gives direction to human experience, human experience will begin to become devoid of its humanity and may result in reckless efforts to heal society through the programatic destruction of self.

Our statements ought not to be construed as a search for a methodological or ideological updating of liberal criminology. Our cry is not for a "new criminology" as a distinct body of knowledge that promises equality within the framework of mechanization or the state. Our objection is not that criminology has been bad or sloppy or methodically disjointed or the work of technicians, but that there *is* a criminology and that the questions of punishment and forgiveness reside outside the grasp of those struggling to answer the questions in their own lives. Our cry, if anything, *is for a different world*, without a criminology or a science of punishment, in which the hierarchical institutions of the state and capitalism are dissolved. Our cry is for the search for meaning of love and harm in the cosmos, in which all are given access to freedom.

The recent trend in criminology has been to latch on to authoritarian marxist principles for meaning and survival (as political and economic elites have historically), but this movement only suggests the desperation of criminologists to avoid the choices that have to be made. For in this marxist vision, neither hierarchy, domination nor the state wither away, but rather, the very consciousness of their presence and destruction. Marxists smash what they see obliquely only to upset further the balance of the universe. We propose a vision of the world where primacy is given not to smashing, but to dissolving, the seeking after compatibility between the rhythms of the human and the natural. Means *is* ends. As scientists we come to command "more of the hidden potential in nature."[3] With imagination we leap to the warmest orbits of the human soul's experience.

LIBERAL CRIMINOLOGY – GRAND MYSTIFIER

As we have come to recognize it, American criminology in its various liberal forms has been a major factor in the persistence of capitalism and the state. Its historical mission has been to mask the activities of the state and state institutions, and their relationship to capitalist institutions, and to develop a belief in these institutions such that political and economic inequalities inherent in hierarchical forms of life remain beneath the surface of proposed realities and unquestionable.

By assuming definitions of crime within the framework of law, by insisting on legal assumptions as sacred, criminologists comply in the concealment and distortion of the reality of social harms inflicted by persons with power. The world is full of strife, war, misery, injustice, crime, exploitation, forced poverty, oppression, rulers, governors and humiliators of all sorts. Specific persons pose serious limitations on our freedom every day because they wish to use each of us as an instrument of *their* "freedom."[4] They surround us with their language, their select concepts and meanings. They secure power and forbid freedom, our right to act in search of personal meaning within a community of concern. They construct hierarchies and institutions to control, manage and teach ideas legitimizing their acts, their freedom to create docile, legally conditioned human animals.

They teach us their values: private property, hierarchy, authority, nationalism-racism, competition. They make it in each person's interest to uphold the political economy which benefits only them. As we come to understand this reality, we must question how it has occurred and continues. Each of us desires health and well-being for ourselves and others. Each of us hopes to minimize the degree of fear, anguish and insecurity experienced each day. Each of us surely does not wish to be ruled, controlled, humiliated or exploited by others. Each of us wishes liberty, the efficacy of freedom.

Yet, while free and responsible for our acts, each of us encounters a world of resistances, limitations on our freedom,

6

our acts.[5] If we all seek the same thing in life and we are fundamentally the same, equally human, then why do we not seek together, collectively, and live as persons helping, mutually aiding one another? Why do so many cheat, rob, steal, kill, control, exploit, govern and humiliate others? Are we not all equally entitled to life, health and liberty? Are life, health and freedom commodities which others may control without question for their own ends? Are controlling, governing, exploiting, humiliating and killing effective means for securing their freedoms, morally acceptable means-ends? If you think so, you must be willing to make your existence one of continuous invading and invasion, of violating others and being violated, of constantly subjecting others to your own thoughts and will and in turn being subjected to the thoughts and wills of others.[6] You must become an object in a universe of objects invaded for others' freedom.[7] You must be able to find friendship and solace in the revenge of invading and violating others over whom you claim authority. If these realities are acceptable to you, then you and your social order will remain "a crazy quilt of authority, of domination and submission, of command and obedience, of coercion and subjection, of rulers and ruled, of violence and force in a thousand and one forms."[8]

All law, authority and institutions of state are based on force, violence and the fear of punishment. Wherever you look in our society, you will find the subtleties and the grossnesses of violence. At home, school, office, factory or field, there is authority directing, ordering, compelling obedience. It is in this atmosphere of force, invasion and violence, authority and obedience, of duty, fear and punishment, that we have all grown up. We now live each day with our teeth on edge, our souls split. We have become so steeped in the spirit of violence that few rarely stop to question whether violence is morally wrong or right. So, accepting of legal and administrative authority and the state, most people simply ask only if the violence is legal, whether the law permits it.[9] Violence has become morality. As people we have become so far removed from conscience that many no longer question the right of the state to kill, to confiscate, to imprison, to invade personal choice at every level of tension.

If an individual, on the other hand, committed the same acts which the state and its agents are doing all the time, s/he would be branded murderer, thief, scoundrel. But as long as the violence is "lawful," under the solemn regency of the state it is approved and people unquestioningly submit to it. So it is not really the use of violence that is objected to, but to persons using violence "unlawfully." Authority, personal values that do not question authority and hierarchy distort or maim a sense of moral justice, a concern with the moral ends of actions.

If you do not believe that controlling, governing, managing, exploiting, humiliating and killing are effective means for securing our freedoms – morally acceptable means-ends – then you must recognize that you must cease to engage in, must resist these activities, must radically alter your values and must begin to search for and develop non-hierarchical living arrangements wherever possible. For to engage these beliefs, one protests against the interests, ideas, beliefs and realities of persons who have power and who are willing to destroy persons to fix the addiction pangs of power.

To engage or challenge these beliefs, of course, meets resistance. Tremendous efforts of control, management and legitimization must burst forth to contain a person's resistance to being controlled, managed, exploited and robbed. To work within neo-capitalist institutions, to produce capital, to maintain a symbolic system that destroys life is to be robbed of the value of being human and any meaningful relationship. To believe in private property and its institutions of mystification is to allow the earth, its natural resources and ourselves to be owned and enslaved. To obey authority – parental, priestly, statist and legal – is to deny the possibilities of one's personal experience, one's freedom to be present in the universe. To allow hierarchy, authority, private property and competition to persist is to ensure the continuance of a struggle among persons of different sexes, races, ages, classes, nations, all. Competition, the struggle to suppress, becomes the soul of life, its produce, the tragedy, the misery.

The conflagrations of state values produce and are themselves social harms and reap only the deprivation of human status. The conflagrations of these values deny human dignity, permitting some to take significant control over the lives of others. At every juncture, the state robs the power to speak about one's personal conflicts sanely. The state has structured its network of institutions such that each person of non-means has come to require the assistance of state workers at every life decision for survival. Each person of non-means is as captive as the coal miner forced to purchase every aspect of life or humanity from the company store. We need mention only the company towns Pullman and Homestead and their robber-baron decadence and inhumanity to provide a vivid picture of caged existence. (Note: Pullman (Chicago) and Homestead (Pittsburg) were towns owned by companies that exploited immigrant workers. The workers worked long hours for meager wages which were more than exhausted paying for food at the company store and rent for company owned housing. The ministers were also company owned. Such a closed economic cycle lined the pockets of Pullman and Marshall Field, Frick and Andrew Carnegie. Such exploitation precipitated worker organizing and strikes, the Haymarket hangings and the Homestead (Pinkerton) war as well as Berkman's attentat on Frick.)

We state, therefore, that it is not the social harms punishable by law which cause the greatest misery in the world. It is the *lawful harms*, those unpunishable crimes justified and protected by law, the state, the ruling elites that fill the earth with misery, want, strife, conflict, slaughter and destruction.[10] War, the health of the state, is the misery most obviously produced, the most cleverly concealed. War is for the protection of monopolist investments, for the control of new markets and natural resources, for the prevention of internal domestic conflict, for the strengthening of nationalism, centralization and legitimacy of the state. For reasons of state, through the technology of state satellites, unmanned bombers and push-button electronics, human persons have been transformed

9

into surplus commodities as warriors and victims – victims of values and interests, authority and property.

Allied to the state in every way, criminology has served as official propagandist, as official charlatan for the liberal state's program of magic. Criminologists have served to legitimize the death-dealing activities of the welfare-warfare state and, by controlling thinking, to characterize them as benign. Through insistence on scientific neutrality, as if they were untainted prophetic judges, criminologists have concealed the hard realities of the relationship between the "benign" welfare state and the malign warfare state. In playing up acts of benevolence, the bread and circuses of the welfare state, the need to humanize techniques of control and managerial strategems, they have avoided and regarded as irrelevant acts of war and bureaucratic destruction and the national purpose of death. It is only recently that we have come to recognize in all its subtleties and complexity the post-industrial despotic character of America, that of *friendly fascism*. (Note: "Post-industrial" refers to the following changes: from production of goods to provision of services; from large organizations to macrosystems; from white-collar work to extended professionalism, and from metropolis to megalopolis. Its despotic character is indicated in that we are ruled by a faceless and widely dispersed complex of warfare-welfare-industrial-communications-police bureaucracies based on a technocratic ideology, a culture of alienation, multiple scapegoats and (as analyzed later) competing control networks. (See Bertrum Gross, "Friendly Fascism: a Model for America," pp. 414–29 in Richard Quinney, ed., *Criminal Justice in America*, Little, Brown, Boston, Mass., 1974.))

If there exists a tension between what is and what could be, if meaning can be found through a cosmic sense, liberal criminology has discovered many forms of avoidance and control to resolve the tensions in favor of state and corporate elites; the principal one is mystification. Criminologists have clothed the state in a unique genre of "benevolent myth." Yet, at the same time, criminologists have decreed with the wrath of a god that persons have no right to personal myths

10

and meaningful forms of personal authority. Far from being their self-proclaimed "value-free" selves, criminologists have coaxed people into cages of myth by insisting on the benign nature of the present political and economic order at every human contact. These are in fact *givens* in the rationalism of the ideology of science, things to be assumed. Then, by calling our attention to "immediate" and "practical" social problems that drain our immediate energies and insights, not only have they legitimized their own presence but they have diverted our attention from the most serious order of crimes, of social harms – those of the state and its military megamachine. Assumptions about themselves are adhered to at any cost, at the imminent risk of the disappearance of the species.

We are fast approaching a point of destruction, it seems. We have fallen into a strange kind of love-hate relationship with the American megamachine and its gallery of social institutions, despite the fact that they continue to reduce the human person and human consciousness to the rudiments of one-dimensional robopaths. This involves the growing dehumanization of people to the point where they become the walking dead. Placed in roles, robopaths have little or no compassion, sympathy or empathy for others. (Robopaths are machine-like simulations of people – their existential state is ahuman. Robopaths have a limited ability to be spontaneous, to be creative, to change direction, to modify their behavior in terms of changed conditions – they do not use their human capacities. Where robopathology is epidemic people normatively commit ahuman and dehumanizing acts. They are part of the plastic social machine that expects limited human compassion, and perpetuates death (see Lewis Yablonsky, *Robopaths: People as Machines*, Penguin, Baltimore, Maryland, 1972).) So deeply shrouded in the rituals of death, so far removed from the signs of death are Americans that it no longer astonishes any but a few to watch the callous editing of human qualities and consciousness. Assent to the various forms of destruction has become a robopathic response. No longer is there a difference between the human and the sym-

11

bolic. All is sacrificed at the altar of the symbolic. Symbols have hypnotized us to the degree that even movements towards freedom do not rid themselves of the symbolic shroud. The new criminologists, the new order of prophets, live, act and speak in nearly pure symbolic regions as if the present were not a reality to be recognized.

As state and capitalist elites continue to rape the poor, children, women, the elderly, the darker skinned, the initiates, the believers in life, America spends any collective energy it might have gazing in awe-struck assent, anaesthetized by the increasing bounty or benevolence for conformity. The state, with its new mandarin of science, the technician-discoverer, with power over technology and what remains of law, attempts to control each area of life, speech and conceptualization that touches upon the make-up and testing of personal reality. Language and public speech are edited, as is conceptual consciousness as early as awareness takes place in the nuclear family, to forge defenses for the indefensible, such that we see public officials making statements such as: "We must distinguish between murder and killing!"

The rape and destruction we are talking about is not the rhythmic ebb and flow of dying that is characteristic in the natural world, where most people make choices about the time and approach to death. Rather it is a forced death, administered by an economy by which a very few prosper from the killing of many, by which a very few deprive the many of human dignity by controlling their food, work, health, resources, ideas and personal style, using them as instruments to their own power ends. The elitist groups not only build and support programs to destroy, but also continue to mask these activities in language and institutions that legitimize their needs and glorify their acts. These are the very institutions that provide the propaganda, control ideas, manage the persons in prisons who disagree, who stand to resist, who say *no* to the kaleidoscope of killing.

If you think we are talking about death and destruction in largely metaphorical terms, you may be a victim of the very processes of violence and destruction we are talking about.

You may be nearing your own extinction. For, unlike natural death, the closer it gets, the less aware people seem to be of its strangling presence and, with all the irony of dying, seem likely to defend the very arms of the strangler. With the same rhetoric and complacency America defends its destruction of natural life, of the carrier pigeon, the sardine, the whale, of rivers, lakes, the atmosphere, of all of us who continue to remain allied to the natural world. There is not only an administrative callousness towards the atrocities we are discussing, towards the starving, towards the violence, towards the dissolution of consciousness. What we are talking about may even seem improbable. The state and its band of public priests, its scientific "value-free" mandarins, have succeeded in putting most subjects into a state of "ethical quarantine"[11] – so that no act, no thought, no life is seen as being related to any other; the moral ends of action are not to be touched upon or experienced, except where they are assumed – in the house with no sign on its door.

One simple irony of all this is that a nation, a people, or culture that has defined itself as "materialistic" has seemingly little concern for the value of material. Value is found in ways to consume and destroy material. America is not fascinated by materials and their beauty, their reflection of creative genius, but with the processes of consumption and destruction, so that new things can be purchased for personal security and patriotic expression. But until the material world is valued for itself, until the physical world is appreciated for its beauty as well as its utility, for its contemplative value as well as its utilitarian value, the development of international mutuality, a merging of eastern and western thought is not unlikely. Fearing an east-west merger on a spiritual level, for through it many would see the folly and true function of the nation-state, western and eastern capitalism continue to reward the abuse and the destruction of material rather than its appreciation. But only when material is valued and contemplated can it be transcended and east and west thus meet beyond the threat of nuclear weaponry, beyond the boundaries of the nation-state, beyond the violence necessary to

13

defend its imaginary, arbitrary and destructive purposes.

As America rages abroad through war and increasingly more subtle forms of colonization, internally it continues to reward the atrocities of civil war in which, for the sake of maintaining elitist power and privilege, the rich manage, instrumentalize, consume the energies of and destroy those not rich; stake a system that itself has gone mad. And as America feels no guilt for its presence of destruction in Southeast Asia, it feels no particular guilt for its continuing hierarchical piling of person upon person. We imprison the young in schools and destructive sex roles, the old in rigid castles of waiting-to-die. Over forty thousand poor White, Black and Spanish-speaking children die each year for lack of pediatric, pre-natal and obstetric care.[12] Meanwhile armies, secret agencies and police control and kill the body and soul with megatechnic armament; the mandarins of medicine, legalisms, and "teaching" engage in mass death of dignity, by denying goodness about the body and the human spirit, ever refusing to engage in the demystification of themselves and those they serve.

Criminologists who have refused to accept this reality, and who have taken a critical stance toward criminology and the criminal justice system, have received the kind of response that we have come to expect and shall continue to expect. They have been refused tenure, ushered out of teaching in universities. At some academic institutions, where marxist and anarchist perspectives have become apparent, and faculty have engaged in "politically embarrassing" actions, there has been a calculated movement to "eliminate or drastically sanitize" the faculties.[13] Universities which depend heavily upon grants from state and corporate foundations are not willing to run the risk of losing their financial status and academic reputation, their crucial role in political education and destruction, their ability to shore up our decadent hierarchical structure for the checking of those who resist.

Those faculty who teach the ethics of collective consciousness and develop affinity work groups among students and community members are in jeopardy because of their failure

14

to secure grants and to write the kind of papers that win acclaim among academic dinosaurs. Unlike their establishment colleagues, they care more for knowledge and people than for insuring the university's status. To the former group, a riot of the desperate, the organizing of women, farm workers, resistance, or any event which dramatizes human deprivation is an opportunity merely for a new grant, additional funds to train automatized technicians and to test more and more methodologies,[14] social experiments and information supplied to state mandarins of control. In this way the university continues the integral role of education in the order of political society by purging from its ranks those with dissenting views. In the presence of instrumentalities such as liberal criminology, it has become a gatekeeper for state domains of control, the value assumptions of hierarchical authority, the necessity of centralized control, the sanctity of private property and war.

That the writings of persons such as Packer, Schwitzgebel, Ervin, Skinner, Wolfgang and Morris are given such serious positive attention in criminology is indicative of the continued fascination with power, control, and the models of the mechanical world. Their thinking insists that man is the center of the universe and the scientist the center of man. And, as the center of the human species, the scientist can and should prescribe what is good and just and how the world and life processes should be managed. Acceptable to the university and its various scientific clubs are ideologies that promote mechanization and technology as sources of control but not those that insist upon the primacy of human experience and the search for meaning. To remain part of the academic scene requires, at its least, submission to a shearing of consciousness that is tantamount to a shearing of one's humanity. To stand by and observe is to participate; passivity is activity; passivity is assent.

THE GREENING OF CONSCIOUSNESS

The greening of consciousness, the rejuvenation of spirit, is neither simple nor painless. As we deal with the ironies of materialism, the destruction and acquisition of materials in a technological-scientific age, we must face the same ironies in the acquisition of consciousness. We can only painfully become aware of self and the rhythms of the natural. To be *becoming*, to be conscious, requires acute mental struggle, struggle requiring the shedding of values, interests, lifestyles and relationships that oppress or divide. It requires a reordering of language and thought and the understanding of a belief system that views each person as absolutely specific and good. It is futile to talk of freedom and possibility if we refuse to accept this.

The problem is that many no longer believe in anything. Many feel no hope for survival, no conception of possible rejuvenation, the possibility of believing in anything or anyone. For many whose belief structures have been obliterated, who have chosen to give up their lives and minds to the designs of the state, contact with another human is their only guarantee that they are in contact with reality.[15] And yet, amid the spiritual and human carnage, there are unfathomed realms which, as William James stated, "forbid a premature closing of our accounts with reality."[16] In the very processes of destruction sprout the liberative seeds of new life.

Perhaps what we have to say sounds like folly or even crime to many people because they are not yet ready to hear these remarks. Nevertheless, we hope to impart with conviction the reality that all forms of the state are obsolete, destructive of the consciousness necessary for the dignity and survival of humankind. We hope to aid in the greening of consciousness to the dialectics of economic and legal oppression, to the dialectics of personal and psychic oppression.

For one, this entails an awakening to both the practical and symbolic functions of the present criminal processing apparatus – the "criminal justice" system. Criminology has helped to dull the consciousness to the political and economic significance of the "justice" machine. Criminologists have preached a prophecy that promises the restoring of harmed relationship, while in fact the justice machine has reflected

16

only the symbolic processing of persons in order to uphold the values of the ruling few. Embodied in law and regulatory bureaucracy, these values are assumed and preached to be non-negotiables in the process of justice. Private property does not become an issue in the courtroom. State power, its shielding of economic elites, is unquestioned by its agents. The "deviants" trotted out by hired hands as symbolic victims of the apparatus are processed for consumption – evil detractors from the good life. The war machine requires the processing of persons as it does goods, automobiles, refrigerators, and facial arrangements. In cages, shafts of light and spirit fall on those with dark skins, with few material possessions, unconventional lifestyles and those who engage in acts or hold beliefs threatening to the interests of the current benefactors/designers of the political order. If you are not in the processes of professing conformity to the present war machine, you run the risk daily of being edited out of the landscape. As long as one of us is victim, we are all victims.

Yet, in these processes, the state is always caught between the immediate interest in ending the threat to its sanctity at hand and the long-range interest in continuing to maximize its legitimacy and thereby limit revolutionary potential.[17] The elite and their dirtyworkers, therefore, respond with acumen to acts which threaten their existence, their power, their interests and which function to dissolve their needed value, while at the same time maintaining their legitimacy under the guise of benevolence.

The prison, the new policy proposals for deterrence that seek "outright" punishment, service the elites by separating the unsafe from society and dramatizing the futility of their lives, while at the same time protecting the interests of those who promote militarism, those who pollute or destroy our natural resources for profit, those who manufacture and promote unsafe, needless products, those who thwart the free organization of persons.[18]

The Catonsville Nine do hard time for burning paper while the corporate-military state remains unchecked for burning the tender skin of children with napalm. Military machines

17

bomb holes into the hillsides of Vietnam, the back and front sides of humankind and remain beyond incrimination. Dick Gregory and Daniel Berrigan dig holes in the White House lawn in protest of the killing and are arrested, jailed, publicly ridiculed and condemned. In the wake of hundreds of thousands of dead Indochinese, few Americans have stopped to mourn or feel any guilt for their acts. Americans and their corporate leaders rather weep over inflation, decreasing profits and the dissolving sense of morality. While humankind screams in hunger for food, for a touch of humanity, the United States government engages its megamachines in building obsolete bombers for over ninety billion dollars. There is no show of guilt, no sensitivity to the gravity of human massacre. Have schools and institutions shackled our consciousness to the extent that we have come to expect cosmic massacre in history as absolute, as if history were outside the humans directing it?

If social scientists have emerged as the market researchers for the corporate state, criminologists have become its locksmiths. Not only do criminologists provide the rationale for the maintenance of the state and its control of dissidents, but they shield the eyes and close the noses of people to the destruction of themselves, of people. They prefer to spend time on researching parking meter fraud and the class and status of immigrants in American pizza shops than the struggles of humanity.

The present movement of *new* or radical criminologists is toward authoritarian marxism and vanguard ideologies but these provide no true alternative to issues of the kinds we are raising. For their own personal acquisition of power, these ideologues would serve to sacrifice the human. It is in each person's awakening to the realities of the world, its miseries, its human condition and to the design and function of all states that meaningful alternatives come. It is a reckoning with the function of criminology and a sharing of the guilt for its part in the masking of the destruction. At the same time, it is an act of demystification of its mission in relation to the state and present economic order. It is an act of speaking out amid the continuing conflagrations of nations and consciousness. It is the recognition of person as good and valuable and the importance of resistance to the continuing conflagrations of personal consciousness set by the state. It is person as actor, as creator responding to the conviction of Gandhi: "Inaction at a time of conflagration is inexcusable . . . when [the] occasion demands speaking-out the whole truth and acting accordingly . . . silence is cowardice."

For criminologists personally, the present movement is an insistence on the need for direct action, on the urgent need to detach our personal lives from the destructiveness of ideological cul-de-sacs and power systems. It is the courage to act to develop alternative living arrangements that contain their separate authenticity. This criminology is an engagement of the human community in ending the processes of disillusion, alienation, dismemberment, and destruction inherent in capitalism and the state, before no restorative measures are possible.[19]

The experiences of "the new criminologists" reveal the necessity for a social consciousness that has a profound concern for questions of power and authority. We agree, but we urge not "the getting into" power or transference of power, but the dissolution of power into forms of relationship that reflect collective consciousness, collective activities. Criminologists must come to recognize as primary the need to know how we come to know, how we come to experience the world about us, how we come to celebrate life while fully aware of our mortality and the inevitability of death. We must entertain an awful sensitivity to the fact that there is no clear beginning, no certain resolution and no obvious method when we begin to ask: Who am I? What is my relationship to other persons, other forms of life? What is death? What is my relationship to the death of other persons, the interference with other forms of life? – and hundreds of other urgent questions.[20]

In the continuing struggle to develop community and social theory, the criminologist begins to develop an awareness that he is part of the world and is slowly divested of the illusion that the real questions of social misery, social harm, life and death can be measured or calculated mathematically. He becomes painfully aware that he has the same problems as those he has studied in the past and that, until those he studies are freed, he is not freed. It is all part of a rather stark process of unmasking that no longer permits the scientific observer in us to remain beyond question, beyond the human. It is a recognition that we must turn scientific inquiry over to the community, toward a collective inquiry into meaning. At the same time, we must be sensitive to the mystery of life, the mystery of human experience, the mystery of a world of mutual aid. As criminology is greened, ruptures and begins to prepare to pass into extinction, its swan song is a honking challenge to legal authority, the state, rationality, objectivity and certainty. It signals the end to legal mythology, to the continuing presence of the state. It signals the end of scientific detachment from the human.

CRIMINOLOGY AS SCIENTIFIC METHOD

Historically, it is not surprising to find statements about justice reflecting the ideology of the state, of law and the existing economic order. The just were always the state. Neither is it surprising to find statements of resistance to this consciousness. But many who have claimed *justice* as their domain of study act as if issues of justice are distinct from issues of freedom, as if issues of freedom can be separated from those demanding quality of life for all. Scientists themselves have been defrauded by the rationale for specialization, the division of labor of the machine economy, and most have abandoned the search for any cosmic sense. Rather than seeking to transcend presently accepted modes of reality in search of meaning, scientists hang on to their black bag of ideological remedies, ministering fraudently to those who were told they needed these remedies to survive. In the context of the liberal state, these black-bag magicians issue forth no statements about the quality of life, but rather about the quality of certain lives, of liberalism, of systems that have no regard for persons. They have accepted the division of the world as it suits the needs of its destroyers rather than its creators. Justice has everything to do with their separate "professional" world views but nothing to do with their personal selves. They are mercenaries of thought for hire, willing to compartmentalize themselves into as many parts as is necessary to do business with minimum interference.

Until today and still continuing, the scientific community has turned the liberative components of science into the deadening repression of the state. Rather than smashing idols that take away clarity of vision, scientists themselves have posed themselves as minor idols (mandarins) and breathe the uneven breath of the saint who considers himself beyond his humanity. The rhythms of the philosopher in the scientist-expert are muted. The history of philosophy and science comes rather to be a "forgetting of being," a shunning of meaning and concern and a contentment with the world of "things to be used."[21] As the science of the rational developed its technics, the things to be used became things to be consumed, to be destroyed and eliminated. And human experiences that do not meet standards of certainty and cannot be measured as "problem" are abandoned as irrationalities. As the nation-state and capital-intensive activities have come to be dependent upon the use of things and ultimately humankind for its survival, more and more is regarded as irrational. For the lush of power, western man has dug into the natural environment, designed needless, wasteful shelves on to which the empty souls of America can crawl to rest and die.

As the so-called experts of life continue to defoil the natural, living world, they also defoil the minds and tongues of its human inhabitants. They control language about what is real, coin and fit words for the kaleidoscope of illusions they design as the capitalist cover-up. Thus we live in a culture in which people have no sense of their position, no ground in the physical world. Geographically, we are aimless wanderers, feet in the air. We have no sense of the patterns of nature, know no names of wildlife, birds, trees and flowers – all of

21

which could disappear from our view without our protest, for they have already passed from our conceptual realities. We, all life, are near the vanishing point, for a human relationship to nature and other forms of life is contingent upon the human understanding of itself. What people do about their ecology depends upon what they think about themselves in relation to everything about them. Human ecology is deeply conditioned by beliefs about our nature and destiny – that is, by spirituality.[22] It is a warped or absent spirituality which "rationally" strip-mines mountains in West Virginia and pulls the hills of trees to their knees. It is the same spirituality which politically and economically controls the lives of those who starve over the next hollow. We must wake ourselves from this sleep, this warped spirituality, to become more intensely aware of the living vibrations of the real world of human and life kind.[23]

Criminology must be seen as an expression of this consciousness, this warped spirituality. Criminology, within the context of scientific rationality, has reflected an almost naive contentment with the assumptions of scientific method. If social scientists are guilty of anything, it is passive acceptance of the domains of inquiry parcelled out to them, the implicit acceptance of the assumptions that justice and freedom are possible in the abstract, within the institutions which give criminology its legitimacy and to which in turn legitimacy is given. Criminologists have committed a crime far graver than we see at first glance, and for which the marxists criticize them. This crime is that of trading the totality of human experience, not merely the lives of prisoners and the different, for that minute portion which can be observed within the framework of the law and scientific method, while simultaneously denying importance to the unmediated realities of human experience, for which science itself is only a refined ideological derivative.[24]

Criminologists especially among social scientists continue to demonstrate an outright rejection, at least a reluctance, to believe that the methodology of science can be viewed in the context of ideology. They behave as if law and the state were absolutes, were the impeccable foundations of *the* correct world, receiving authority by way of some absolute divine right. Slavishy following the dictates of scientific method they have repeated the error of the physical and mechanical scientists to whom "the human personality was an embarrassment to the new conception of 'objectivity'."[25] As with the theoretical sciences of technology, the whole range of social sciences fixed themselves on eliminating the "irrational" from the required predictability of everyday systems of industrialization, institutionalization and control.

Though criminologists have been concerned with social relationship, social organization and disintegration, the underlying philosophy of thought has been essentially the same as that of the physical sciences. People and the struggles of the human community are seen as "out there", as objects or "things" that can be viewed and reviewed as under a microscope, dissected and stuck back together as could the elements of a chemical compound. Even the fascination with the psyche is with its compound of elements rather than with a person struggling to be human among many and continuing contradictions.

The incessant apologia of social scientists that their methodologies are value-free comes from their unwillingness to consider their own mode of thinking about the world, to consider themselves as part of the one world of human struggle. They demonstrate little questioning of the sources of authority that dictate who is to be observed and controlled. The "moral scientist" could seemingly be separated from the "observing scientist", a dissection of self that scientists like J. Robert Oppenheimer were to bemoan in themselves in later years. And, if we can cite Einstein, Szilard and Wiener as scientists who rejected atomic research because morality and the state had become one, we can recount but few criminologists who have come to view criminological science as police action.

Rather than deal with their assumptions about person and life and the natural world, the scientist-criminologists continue to assume the benevolence of the cloak of rationality, observation and policy to define the sick and withering members of the world. Then they proceed to hang out shingles advertising their messianic nature, their secret priesthood to save and restore, for the right price, those whom their research and policies set up. But as they have become more vociferous about their authority, their mandarin status, they have begun to lose their flock, to be without convinced believers. They have become beyond belief, beyond the human, in exchange for becoming a source of ideological comfort for the stomping elite. They are losing the pool of believers not even to alternate visions but to passivity and fright.

As criminology has become less and less critical, the more available and/or saleable its services have become for the social order as it is rather than as it might be. Many criminologists still see the world of "social problems" to be the world before their scientific, legally corrected and state-corrected eyes. In assigning a prophetic quality to their vision, by assuming the correctness of that vision, the correctness of the current institutions, the correctness of their assessment of the human condition, and current forms of misery, they seek the causes and remedies of crime, disorder and misery in people, those whom the law, the elite, define as socially harmful. For continued membership in the elite class, the scientist pays dues by mitigating the guilt of the elites by providing scientific rationales for the destruction of various scapegoat groups. Given people to look at without an historical, relative view of law and illegality, criminologists see abnormalities as conflicts residing within the soul, the person, rather than within the ideas, values, interests, authority of the powerful, and crime as one form of resistance to these ideas, interests and persons. Focus on conflict within the soul avoids the critical issues, for it denies that deviance is authentic, an extension of the powerful, controlling classes. Such a perspective denies that deviance is the expression of the consciousness of injustice, manifesting itself as infrequent, slumbering, smoldering revenge on the manufacturers of injustice, but more frequently manifested on self and others of similar state to oneself.

An atomizing economy, a disenfranchising, politicizing, ruling, managing, centralizing order has paid the criminologist well to diagnose, classify and treat personal misery, subjective injustice and resistance as personal pathology. What behavior the criminal law cannot contain within its domain to hunt out "the pathological", institutionalized psychiatry and social work, in their sheepish submission to positivistic modes of thinking, seal tight. Alternative realities, even those not communicated or shared, while authentic expressions of what is possible in the realm of public issues and organizational possibilities, are declared private, personal matters. To state the collective importance of alternative realities is to invite public defamation from the state. The social structure within which violence, destruction and the use of human beings as instrumentalities is institutionalized, built into its very interstices, is a structure within which the sensitive are the first to be a part of the holocaust and death-dealing. Those who seek meaning for their personal lives are the first to be acted upon. Those who retreat, bail out or rebel, for whom no community of meaning exists, become the ready victims of the one forced reality of the state. To go some *place* else is of little avail, for statist oppression is universal, to go *some mind* else is, for it is a place to shed one's social identity, to find some meaning in life, safe from the continuing holocaust. Each act of the state puts people in the "double bind" where they are faced with the rejection of self for the sake of an idyllic institutional permanence that exists for the lubrication of the American war machine.

CHICAGO CRIMINOLOGY

The work of those criminologists who have been called members of the Chicago school is an important part of our present statement, for the Chicagoans provide us with a basis for establishing collective consciousness whereby no person or group suffers from ideological oppression. Situated on the doorsteps of the city's poverty and squalor, these criminologists took the issues of scarcity and economics into theoretical consideration. However, scarcity to them was urban scarcity, the scarcity of the neighborhoods, the scarcity of the endless americanization of immigrants. Boundaries and the competition for space and resources were taken into account, but only within the context of ethnic groups fighting among themselves for available resources, for space in the thick broth of the host culture's melting pot.

The Chicagoans demonstrated a sensitivity to the regularity of certain kinds of social activities within certain natural boundaries and their impact on the social ecology of the city, but not on the ecology of the natural environment. Scarcity of resources for them was not the scarcity of nations, populations under capitalism. With the ruins of industrialization spread before their eyes, the Chicago theorists saw the immediacy of solving problems of urban poverty and decay as more pressing and humane than the need for the development of theory extending analysis to an international economic and political context.

To the Chicago School it is possible to trace the ancestry of the parochial technicians of liberal criminology, as well as the benevolent criminology of the present welfare state. The scientism of criminology manifested itself increasingly in sophisticated methodologies and social management programs which could extend the tentacles of the host culture and control the crime problem of the immigrants. For most Chicagoans, the problem of justice was a problem of people management, responded to in the form of a "well-regulated, stable and humanitarian system of criminal justice under the present economic and political arrangements."[26]

American cities came to be managed like American game farms as the sociologists and criminologists measured the depletion and shifting of resources, but always within the rule structure of the game warden.

But fairness to the Chicagoans demands an account of their position toward those whom they studied and struggled for. Unlike some marxists who see "deviant low life" as having no power potential for revolution, as the unwashed who someday might be saved, the Chicagoans saw "them" as no different from the rest of the social world of the city's various subcultures.

They might characterize "deviants" as "troubled", but they were troubled "persons," not statistics and not, as some marxists assert, without historical future or mission. Those subcultural groups which were initially characterized as disorganized or without effective organization were, on observation, discovered either to have a *different* organizational structure or to be "disorganized" from the perspective of the observed themselves, in that the latter were unable to prevent high rates of unemployment, infant mortality and crime on the streets. Both structural and cultural factors militated against the development of community consciousness. Recent immigration, rural migration, economic segregation, heterogeneity and mobility interacted to repress community consciousness in certain natural areas. In the absence of a consistent set of cultural standards (ones acceptable to members of dominant groups), social reform could bring the beneficial effects of the host culture – homogenization, consensus and control. Yet, the Chicagoans did not always think the way of life of the dominant group was morally superior. They did not always conceive of the "deviant" phenomenon of their research as simple or pathological. In fact, through intensive observation, it was discovered that all ways of life were complex, that the ways of life of the hobo, gang member and taxi hall girl were exciting, adventurous and undertaken with autonomy.

The Chicagoans did not always impute pathology to the ways of life of the persons they studied, invoking the correctional model.[27] In fact, those researcher-observers most faithful to the reality they were portraying, who constructed a dense and detailed description of the subject's way of life in the subject's own language, were least likely to impute pathology to these subjects.[28] Not only were these Chicagoans those least involved in the professional world of the sociologist (scientist) but also they never recommended remedies, policies or reforms which would have hospitalized, incarcerated or treated the persons studied.[29] The process of close observation allowed them to appreciate the complexity, diversity, and authenticity of different lifestyles.

But while these Chicagoans illustrate the liberating aspects of research[30] and, through contrast, the structural meaning of developing interests in the position of the scientist,[31] other factors as well were at work in their observations. Primary among these factors is the finding that the decisive factor affecting the definition of the observed phenomena as abnormal was not the distance from conventional social practices but the extent to which the phenomenon was organized as a powerful counterculture at odds with deeply held values and norms.[32]

The blind spot of the Chicagoans was in not taking *their own world* into account. Politicians and reformers could be viewed within the same kind of hustling framework as pimps but somehow the scientist was regarded as beyond it all. If the pimp was a hustler and the reformer of the pimp also a hustler, was not then the observer of such activities also a hustler, or did overseeing life through scientific methodologies have a special purifying effect, rendering the observers above it all? While all groups and persons studied were seen to struggle in the same world, somehow it was the scientist himself who became the deified one, the other-worldly one who could save and reform.

It is at this point that any radical criminology must come to grips with its liberal-reform past stemming from the Chicagoans as well as marxist alternatives. Social revolution cannot occur if the future powerful elites (scientific mandarins or political mandarins) are the objects of our hope, for we are the objects of their control. Revolution is for everyone and must take place not only *for*, *with* and *among* those with broken hopes and dreams but also among those with bent noses, broken faces, torn and crooked bodies, who may not have immediate revolutionary potential but have the potential to engage in the struggle to be human. If criminology is to become a realistic part of the social world, it must be the social world that exists now, the struggles of all persons in the course of imposed power and reform. This means to engage in the struggle to transcend the liberal traditions of the Chicagoans and at the same time the power alternatives of the authoritarian marxists. To become part of the social world requires a denunciation of authority, elitism and all the unappreciation of life that floods our souls. It means the construction of alternative arrangements for living, for negotiating the rhythms of the natural world.

Those who would "teach" justice in the social world must also begin to see themselves as part of the present system of symbolism. They must recognize the need to relate issues of justice and freedom to collective or shared responsibility, which is to tear away at the supports of hierarchy and privilege. It is to confront statists, elites, and expose their relationships, values and functions; it is to unmask social structures which perpetuate and create social harms, atomize life, colonize and oppress, and attempt to dull consciousness, creativity and spontaneity. At the same time it is to unmask oneself, to expose the residues of personal violence and forms of personal oppression and to be in touch with the continuing demands of our own biorhythms.

THE END TO DETACHMENT AND RATIONALITY

People's thinking about the world has consequences for how they come to know and behave in that world and how they come to appreciate life and life processes. How people experience the world leads them to make judgements about that world and its peoples and their own value and purpose in it. A criminology that seeks an end to detachment, and involvement in organic processes, must reflect on its own doing and thinking. It is an expression of the conviction that, as Paul Goodman has stated, "our problems are *not* technological and sociological, they are moral and political," and cannot be calculated in what is euphemistically described as objective data. Criminologists cannot *collect* data but must *be* the data that reveal their course of action. Therefore, a view of the world that is real cannot be proposed unless the world of the criminologist is real and experiential. This, at the very least, entails a critical view of one's own way of thinking and experiencing.

For the scientist this process is risky because it entails examination of *explanation* as a way of thinking about oneself and the world and its limitations. It is the criminologist-technician applying to himself, his beliefs and lifestyle, the critical processes he has applied to others, "for the sake of truth," for the sake of control. It means no longer viewing the world as dualistic – as composed of subjects and objects; the criminologist is faced with being a part of the world of experience to find "there is only one breed of men." "He finds that the knower's knowing of himself – of who, what and where he is – on the one hand, and of others and their social worlds, on the other, are two sides of a single process."[33] The kind of thinking process we are talking about, of itself, thinks of the world in terms that extend beyond the structured confines of what rationality will allow. There is present for the knower a sensitivity to mystery that is fully appreciative of the dialectics and contradictions of human experience. We find ourselves as having only one world in which to struggle to be human, in which to resolve our convictions.

The rationalist who looks out at the world as an entity "out there", when he finds no methodological evidence, resorts to disbelief. Things that empiricism cannot explain are labeled as irrational, for these unexplainable phenomena not only threaten one's hold on the objective world but destroy the illusion of objectivism of a reality quite apart from consciousness.[34] But "the error of empiricism," Gabriel Marcel wrote, "is to take experience for granted and to ignore the mystery; whereas what is amazing and miraculous is that there should be experience at all."[35]

For the rational technician who has survived on defining and "ordering" the world of the irrational, the world of experience is a rejection of the consuming icons of certainty and a request to give up priesthood for a world where "at first sight things do not go together."[36] It is immersion in what Keats described as negative capability "when man is capable of being in uncertainties, mysteries, doubts, without an irritable reaching after fact and reason."

To date, this kind of thinking and engagement of human experience has been the realm of the poet and artist. Through it, each comes "to let each impression and each germ of feeling come to completion quite in itself . . . beyond the reach of one's own understanding."[37] Contrary to the world of the ordering, dominating and destructive scientist, that of the poet is respectful of things, of human diversity and of the ideas and perceptions created by past generations as expressions of correct possibilities of these epochs. The poet is always conscious of his own responsibility as creator of new insight, in casting original light on things that are.[38]

As criminology approaches extinction, criminologists of the state must come to an awareness of the influences of the world of the state, its harms, miseries, destruction and control – of its disrespect for the diversity of the meaning of life created by past and present generations. Criminologists of science must recognize that their detachment and rationality act as a continual invalidation of human sentiments and promote an acceptance of the hierarchical order as given, prohibiting people from experiencing their personal worlds. As criminology approaches extinction, unknown realms are revealed, the seeds of new realities.

ALTERNATIVES

The immediate roots of the rupture of criminology, the development of radical criminology, can be traced to the experience of criminologists in the political anti-war dramatizations of the sixties. Those criminologists who personally became part of the struggles to resist police action could no longer be bound on an "academic level" by the arbitrary domains of criminology, when the professed objectivity of criminology could provide no meaning for their struggles in a community of resistance to the military machine. For many of us these experiences began to erode the possibility of engaging in any scientific work that professed political or social neutrality. Concern and thought has begun to shift from the limited vision of technical control to the realm of social possibility

31

and theories of life that do not exclude human experiences.

In criminology, the movement for a new society and the development of critical social theory readily allied itself with marxism. Having an acceptable academic tradition, marxism provided an immediate vision and possibilities of thought. Anarchism, unwelcomed even among the intellectual community, was thought to have been buried in the blood and dust of the Spanish Revolution, thanks to the spadework of statists and marxists. The writings, lives, actions and visions of Godwin, Proudhon, Kropotkin, Bakunin, Tolstoy, Berkman and Goldman were mostly unknown. They remain unfamiliar to most in the discussion of alternate social arrangements today.

As criminologists up to now have turned to marxism as the only alternative mode of existence, we state flatly that it is not that anarchism is an alternative. In fact, we question whether especially authoritarian marxism is any alternative at all – in theory or practice – for the state, hierarchy, elitism and materialism are part and parcel of its visions. Given the nature of the alienation and fright caused by the technological megamachine, centralization and control, anarchism is an alternative by which human community can be restored. Given the nature of a post-scarcity society which technology has allowed, anarchism becomes an alternative for fostering quality of life for all.

The radical criminologist cannot remain content with only a *critical* philosophy. The liberating force behind radical criticism is not the criticism but "the movement from revelation to the development of a new consciousness and a new life in which we transcend the established existence."[39] Human persons are believers and those who begin to disbelieve know that they cannot deny for too long, for through continued disbelief in the world comes denial of human possibilities. Authoritarian marxism is essentially denial of belief in anything that is beautiful for in the long run it is willing to smash whatever disagrees ideologically. Human possibility cannot be found in acts of negation or smashing but in being present to the world. It is, also, one thing to engage in acts of demysti-

32

fication, another to actively practice one's vision of community and one's cosmic sense. It is an act of existence that involves an extension of self toward what is unknown and is not yet, so that new possibilities may come about and new explanations be offered for things that are.

Therefore, we cannot dismiss as "irrational" or nonexistent what we cannot readily understand, categorize or count, for we may be discounting the source of our potential being. If within the mechanical realm of science the human personality was a source of embarrassment, within the the realm of new vision and thinking human experience is the center. The mechanical world must be viewed only as a force that can facilitate liberation, freedom and meaning, that supports personal receptivity to the mystery of human experience. Machines must not be used to destroy others as they are in our present order. They should be used as life-giving support, not for the extension of control, statism and profit.

It is no longer realistic to respond to the domination of an advanced technological order in terms of "worker exploitation" and "class analysis." The process of disintegration and rupture we are witnessing sheds its fallen hairs on all persons, values and institutions. It invades human consciousness and every human endeavour at every juncture. When Marx presented the theory of immiseration, he saw an increasing impoverishment accruing to workers as capitalists competed. But what he could not see was the development of state capitalism, the planned, controlled economic and political enslavement of all. He spoke, therefore, of the preconditions of liberation, not of the conditions.[40] We are today engaged in realizing a "post-scarcity consciousness" which is neither issue-oriented nor drowned in abstraction, but which seeks community and quality of life for all in the present. It reflects the present actualization of the concepts of mutual aid, spontaneity, economic freedom and justice. At the same time it requires dissent from violent ideologies of any sort and the recognition that one's means are one's ends. To espouse violence of any sort is to share in violence, regardless of collateral rhetoric about relationship and community, for it is movement away from mutual aid, away from the very conditions that foster successful human evolution (Note: The issue of the use of violence in bringing about social change is extremely complex. Stuart Christie has insightfully addressed this question in the introduction to this book. The definition of what is violent itself is problematic. At the risk of not seeing the social changes we would like to bring about, our position is one of nonviolence. We take the side of principle in the power-principle dialogue. For us the critical question is: If you utilize violent means how do you do so without institutionalizing violence? If violence is acceptable, how do you break through the cycle of violence? If some violence is and some is not acceptable, for whom and when is it not? This seems to be the state's position – violence for reasons of state is acceptable, violence against the state is not. To us an atmosphere of trust is undermined by violence; people become distanced; understanding is diminished; the cycle of violence is unbroken. Yet, we understand fully the actions of Sabate, of Berkman, of Lovejoy's nuclear war, and of so many others. As these issues involve both personal and collective ethics we do not assume our position is necessarily *the* path others must take. Perhaps a diversity of paths, positions and actions are situationally required or necessary for revolutionary process to have an institutional base and yet continue as a process.)

An assessment of what is possible for humankind must take into account the extraordinary social possibilities of our time, social possibilities created by the same machines that have engaged in our oppression. We are now on the threshold of being able to provide for all. With a post-scarcity technology, there is no longer any "social rationale for property and classes, for monogamy and patriarchy, for hierarchy and authority, for bureaucracy and the state."[41] We finally can create the institutions in which poverty and elitism have no meaning. We must begin to drive away the fears of scarcity in Americans and enlighten them as to the collective consciousness necessary to handle the expression of plenty.

The anarchist alternative we are exploring implies the need

34

for a radical definition of life. This entails a radical redefinition of work and human needs. Moreover, anarchism seeks a reworking of what constitutes quality of life for everyone. This extends beyond work to the spiritual and cultural elements of person and society. In this redefining we recognize that experiences and ideas are the foundation of life and social arrangements their creations. To change social arrangements, a change must occur in our experiences and ideas, in how we experience the world. To change our notions about quality of life for everyone we must prepare by educating ourselves to the justice and practicability of a social life based on liberty and economic equality. If we wish to live without authority and compulsion, we must experience cooperation, reorganize our affiliations and begin to establish new human values that reflect cooperative arrangements. We must learn to respect the humanity of each fellow human, neither invading nor coercing anyone, we must learn to consider each person's liberty as being as sacred as our own, to respect each person's freedom and personal style, to forswear compulsion in any form. We must learn to understand that the cure for the possible harms and miseries of liberty is not less but more liberty, that liberty is not the offspring but the parent of order.[42] If the preparation is not undertaken, a new foundation constructed, then merely a new form of authority, hierarchy, state and property will be established. The revolution must begin with individuals reconstructing themselves, changing their lifestyles, providing moral examples, acting on their beliefs, exercising their freedom, struggling to be human.

We live in the time Heidegger described as the time of the double knot. The old gods have died but have not yet been taken offstage. The new gods have not yet arrived. If there is a community of believers ready to respond with conviction, their readiness does not reside in their yearning for more gods, gods of a different color. Our present effort is to take away the masks of the institutional gods of capitalism, law and the state, and to warn those who struggle to be human without a collective conscience of the certain extinction awaiting them, all of us.

35

SUMMARY

Inquiries regarding the question of crime have been segregated from those regarding the state and our struggle to be human. Such a severing has served to mask the deadening force of hierarchical and exploitative relationships and to suppress the possibility of human community. Lawful harms, those protected by laws, states and elites, pervade humankind with misery, want, strife, conflict and destruction. Yet, to harm another person in any manner (robbery or law) is to continue this cycle of exploitation and control. Thus, while the earth is plundered for resources, our human soul is stripped of spirituality. An exclusive and unidimensional valuing of detachment and rationality has served to promote an acceptance of hierarchy and to continuously invalidate human experience and sentiment. Without such sentiment and spiritual rejuvenation we cannot realize that we create our social institutions and that to change them we must change our experiences and feelings. If we wish to live without authority and compulsion, we must feel comiseration and experience mutual aid and community. It is only then that we can consider each person as sacred and break through the cycle of harm, diminishment and separation.

Responsibility

What is the way to change our life?
Where do concerns begin?
Rebel movements are – a farce!
The change comes from within.

The leader cannot smear on truth
And spread it with a knife.
I must make the thought and search
To reshape this one life.

The rebel movement feeds the few
And starves the teeming crowd.
The rebel leader orates lies
To calm and crush the proud.

When each and all have seen the light,
One flick will set aright
The horrors in milleniums
Of terrors, wars and fright.

So rose the mighty Russian, German and Finn.
Before them, all of Europe; after, tortured Spain.
No need of leaders had they then
And they will rise – by self – again.

Smashed can be all government
If each one finds the way
To set aside the many wrongs,
Permit no Lenins to betray.

The factory will guide itself
In "agree" and not in "told".
Each one and group is free to act
In collective act made bold.

Each man a leader in himself,
For responsible behavior.
Himself a power in all things
And no one else his savior.

Thus, crush the power of all wrong.
Cultivate the young.
Educate the stupid ones
The great New Day is sprung!

Hryhori Nestor Rudenko

From Richard Rudolph, *Give Me Soil to Fly In*, (ed.) Dennis Sullivan, Baobab Books Publishers Voorheesville, New York, 1977, p.26.

1 Law: An Instrument of Authority

LAW IS THE INVERSION OF PERSON AND COMMUNITY

Each of us is on a journey to free ourselves of interior ghosts, a brood of fears that erodes our power to experience reality and that translates our dreams into folly. These ghosts reflect our rent self; the means that we take to become whole within determine to what extent we can begin to deal with our existence within the framework of a collective consciousness. Whenever our dreams are thwarted or denied validity, the ghosts become our prisons, become vile absolutes that bind us from resolving the contradictions that appear each day.

The function of law historically has been to deny some people the right to their personal journey, to detain us, by demanding that we resolve our contradictions within the confines of law and the state. In fact, the presence of law itself signifies that there are no valid contradictions to one's life that *it* does not specify, that there is no individuality and therefore no possibility of collective experiences. Law prohibits us from freeing ourselves, experiencing ourselves in the struggle to be human, so that we are left with the option to translate ourselves into slaves of a symbolic or cultural ideal, to live in a cave of shadows that mask the economic and political realities of a destructive elite. When this sedimentation sets in, we become the historical ghosts from whom we are struggling to free ourselves. We deny ourselves our spiritual homes and our ability to become part of the process of creation. We are the makers of the world, but with law we come to deny ourselves our own creative magic.

We must be aware, therefore, of the often subtle mystification processes of law and how these processes impinge upon and deny our individuality. By demystifying legal processes, we come to understand our personal contradictions and begin to grasp the meaning of collective consciousness which claims that law is unnecessary. We come upon the beauty of the world without requiring its possession or destruction. Law at its foundation implies that there is no beauty; there is only ugliness and evil, requiring a watching or power over the universe. There is, in law, no receptivity to the movements of the universe because there is no receptivity to personal movements. To proclaim the goodness of persons and of the universe in an economic and political order that succeeds and sustains itself on the belief of universal evil is to invite the wrath of the producers and possessors of legal and economic power.

Some fundamental recognitions about law are necessary. We must recognize that laws and administrative decisions which are collectively established are not necessarily the will of any individual. When they reflect the will of some or of many, still others are made subject. The personal journey of these subjected persons is denied or aborted because it contradicts the will of the decision-makers. Bakunin:

> "Even in the most democratic countries, the people really obey not laws which they make themselves, but laws which are made in their name, and . . . to obey these laws means nothing else to them than to submit to the arbitrary will of some guarding and governing minority or what amounts to the same thing, to be freely slaves."[1]

To accept law, therefore, is to accept a reality in which there is the imposition of person upon person. It is to accept the reality of enslavement, the plantation of the welfare state. It is to accept the division of the world into parts that translate into subjects and objects, and the mechanisms to manage this hierarchical division, denying autonomy to everyone. It is the continued acceptance of this world of subjects and objects that has lead to what Heidegger has described as humankind's forgetfulness and misunderstanding of being, of our own rhythmic existence. With thinking that assumes distance, hierarchy and eventual destruction, our relationships have become devoid of meaning. Law mythologizes all this, creating a greater misunderstanding of our existence. It proposes, under the pain of force, that the state is the only worthy redeemer, and denies the value of human experience.

Seemingly, we continue to stand for this artificial division of the world into parts and hierarchy without fully realizing how such thinking serves to divide our own persons into parts and to scatter these parts upon the human junk heap. As if in a daze, the human community has become preoccupied with a level of existence in which it continues to forfeit greater portions of its human franchise to the administrative control system of the welfare state. Our present economic and political system allows only for the franchise of submission, submission to the contrived benevolence of a military state where the symbolic takes precedence over the human, where law and the state and its panoply of intoxicating institutions prevail over human experience and our overtures to freedom. Arising with this process is a mythology that suggests that community and collective consciousness are either absurdities or can arise without a struggle from the institutional abstractions and/or the power-oppressive relationships embodied in law.

Our misunderstanding of being has brought us to the point where it has nearly become impossible to speak of justice or of freedom that does not have its ground in law. To begin to search for meaning in this impersonal control system which resides outside the sphere of human experience is to preclude from the human struggle so many possibilities that we come upon our humanity "estranged from its authentic possibilities."[2]

If we expect law to give meaning to the human struggle, we are at the same time stating that the human person is superfluous. We cannot expect to control life and experience from without, and at the same time expect to find meaning within. Law requires that we give up the possibility of real experience

41

within the context of community for the abstractions of the state and the booty of conformity. Each is always forced to choose between his humanity and the abstractions of the state.

Beginning with law, we end with law, for discussion of justice and freedom never quite get beyond the mechanics of legal and administrative processes. Questions of life and life opportunity wind up in tortuous arguments about the intricacies of legal and administrative ritual and their power payoff for those involved. Discussion never reaches a context in which it is questioned whether law is necessary for the human struggle, whether it is destructive of our struggle to free ourselves – as if human experience of itself were deficient and requiring some external force to be tacked on to control or redeem it.

The crux of the matter is more the reverse, whether in fact the human community can survive if law and the state are allowed to persist any longer. Rather than solidifying a community of believers, law instigates a state of cultural disbelief. It turns self away from self and experience, away from collective relationship, away from the whole of the natural world. In a state of shame the human person hobbles about, denying his own validity, expending human energies in dealing with the inhuman power oppression by the few the law serves. The institutions of law and the state, which purport to provide harmony and meaning, become the very agents of human destruction, creating disbelief in the possibility of ever carving a way into the real.

If we are concerned about quality of life we must demythologize law and its philosophical bases. We must admit the need for a new starting point for our thinking about freedom, human relationship and the world. We must be capable of beginning with a kind of thinking that does not accept hierarchical thinking as given, a world of subjects and objects, persons as parts. We must be critical of forms of authority that have a history outside community. Gabriel Moran:

"We must begin to look to human experience for whatever is to

42

be found. No limits are to be set at the beginning or the end for what might somehow be in, with or under experience."[3]

For us, to begin with experience is to no longer frighten away the possibilities within, to no longer turn our thoughts, our faces away from life. It is to no longer remain resigned to the domination of a mythology that destroys and to no longer accept passively the injection of a drug that stultifies possibility. It is to no longer be resigned to promises of a consensual world in which the sanctity of the individual is frowned upon from the outset, in which we are required under threat of violence to forfeit all that is personal. If, like Bakunin, we react to the world we see in the language of enslavement, it is an expression of sensitivity to the oppression of forms of authority that compel the spirit to serve the icons of abstraction, symbol and power, and to make mockery of reason.

All forms of domination of the individual must be displaced, as they deny liberty and responsibility to the individual, recall persons from their own sense of reality and force upon them alternative realities that have their foundation, not in the experiences of the human but in the symbolic.

If law is divisive, there is little sense in continuing to seek after more law or additional ways for law to survive. Post-industrial society's shouts for law 'n order are in essence shouts for relief from the oppression of a world of absolutes that have atomized humanity. The irony is that these incantations for relief bring only more division and greater doses of mystification and personal suffering. The absolutes of law and the state swallow the incanters in the very expression of their suffering. Law persists, people sit in the mire of the belief that all is evil. Celebration comes only in swallowing and destruction, for through these rituals of death-dealing we come to cyclicly support the belief that there is no goodness in the human person.

LAW IS DOMINATION

The modern state is a most ominous form of domination

because of its system of force and intrigue, its law, police, and judges. As the human community struggles to solidify and gain support for its struggles of belief in collectivity, the state's systems of actors strive to shift and tear down human supports, thereby removing people not once but many times from the uncertainties of their humanity. The modern state attempts to make the human appear as illusion. Its systems of actors attempt to reify an institutional rather than experiential response to living. And when the conditions of the institutional system are objected to or challenged as mythical, force is used to squelch the emerging infidel. At each juncture, law serves as the mythical justification. With its system of penal laws, administrative rules and sets of ceremonies which serve to enshrine its legitimacy, state power cultivates a sense of righteousness about itself and its necessity.

Behind the instruments of threat and symbol lies monopolized force, the coercive power to compel compliance. Yet the executors of raw power, the police, the military and the bureaucracy, are for the state a last resort, as their bold presence cuts through the fog of legitimacy and dispels the myth of self-government, of the people as the state. The modern state is thus two-faceted, on the one hand dispensing benevolence to seek compliance and on the other readily resorting to raw force when benevolence fails to gain submission. The state conditionally rewards those, persons or communities, who would accept its absolutes, those who would accept its division of the world. It uses force against those who would challenge its ideology, its international and internal control strategies.

Social custom, religious dogma and moral codes are yet more subtle forms of domination which, like education and official propaganda, are harnessed by the state to perform as ancillary functions of law. They provide extremely effective, subtle forms of obedience, allowing the heavy haze that hides the state and its purposes to remain intact. Countering the active expression of community and relationship, these forms of domination help to mystify, to dominate consciousness in the form of community and collective activities. As forms of

44

domination, they ultimately serve to exile, to cast out. By their intertwined relationship to economic institutions and the state, they prohibit a common memory of the past, common dreams of what might be. They clothe the human community in darkness, proclaiming to a dying community that it lives. State propaganda is so intense that any attempt to transcend its limits is the work of a lifetime.

Legitimacy

Support for the legitimacy of the modern state is increasingly pervasive. It can be found in the monopolization of the media by the ruling class, the manipulation of the ideology of nationalism and patriotism, the institutionalization of religious beliefs, the hierarchical and authoritarian traditions of the unionization of labor, the traditions of tolerance, civil liberties, reform and political competition within the arena of non-critical interests and values, the selective spread of relative prosperity, and in the socializing functions of literacy, educational institutions and the nuclear family.[4] At the very outset of human experience, state values are transmitted, and throughout one's struggles to liberate oneself, state institutions in a variety of forms are found to reinforce these transmitted values. Sanctions are located at every juncture to systematically stigmatize, isolate and punish the non-believers, those who would dissent through what they discover as real persons.

The root from which non-elites legitimate the existing social order can be found in the capacity of the human spirit to psychologically adjust within concentration camp or current life conditions. The root can also be found in learned and reinforced conceptions of "human nature" or a philosophy of person which sets limits to thinking and to experiencing.

The Social Contract Myth

Philosophical constructs are perhaps the strongest hold of the modern state or any state, for it is at this level that the state

45

receives its most formidable form of legitimacy by setting limits on thinking and experience. The ground for thinking of the modern state can be traced to the philosophy of person constructed by Hobbes and the other social contract writers, who assert that all persons are by nature self-seeking, that people are motivated in their self-serving acts by pleasure and deterred by pain; that acts toward freedom are acts of selfishness.

Such a conception of human nature envisions persons creating a social order which would in fact *order*, thereby providing security and protection from one another. For Hobbes, "the solitary, poor, nasty, brutish and short" nature of human existence would continue to yield a war of all against all, unless there was a superior power, the state, to prevent it.[5]

The justification for government thus rests on a contract which each person "signs," yielding his or her freedom in lieu of restraints necessary for the sake of peace. Laws from this perspective are, according to Beccaria:

> "the conditions under which men, naturally independent, united themselves in society. Weary of living in a continual state of war, and of enjoying a liberty which became of little value, from the uncertainty of its duration, they sacrificed one part of it to enjoy the rest in peace and security. The sum of all these portions of the liberty of each individual constituted the sovereignity of a nation; and was deposited in the hands of the sovereign, as the lawful administrator.
>
> "But it was not sufficient only to establish this deposit. It was also necessary to defend it from the usurpation of each individual, who would always endeavor not only to take away from the mass his own portion, but to encroach on that of others. Some motives, therefore, that strike the senses, were necessary to prevent the despotism of each individual from plunging society into its former chaos. Such motives are the punishments against the transgressors of the laws."[6]

Yet this, the Hobbesian view of humankind, has not singly been sufficient to legitimate the social contract. Rousseau, though believing the character of natural man to be good, argued that self preservation required men to contract out their private rights. "The Rousseau paradox is that to gain survival entails a loss of humanity. Rights are swallowed up by obligations. The state absorbs civil society. Natural (good) man is outflanked and outmaneuvered by society."[7] Order is created by social contract with the state and preserved by the institutions of the state.

Mutual Aid

In contrast to this account of history, philosophy and mythical contract is the little-noticed reality that order is and has been constructed through mutual aid, cooperation, spontaneity and peace. There has never been a contract struck between persons and the state. No one signs a contract when born, yielding liberty to state obligations. A truly valid and meaningful social order is one which is voluntarily constructed by each person freely entering relationships with others, constantly renewing or dissolving agreements based on each person's own desire.

To claim that persons must give up a part of themselves to government to watch, as if in sacred escrow, is to state that people must give up the essence of the human struggle, that they must become passive slaves to government and at the same time to their existence by never facing the contradictions of existence and foregoing the existential experience of being present to oneself and others.

Law, cajoling and coercing persons into various institutional mazes under the guise of its falsely universalistic criteria, pays no heed to individual sanctity, and thus, whatever its form, cannot help but invade each person's liberty. Law invades each person's personal struggle, checking the steps he or she takes to cope with aloneness and suffering. Invalidating human experience at its most basic level, law requires persons to yield personal dimensions to the state, leaving persons one-dimensional. Clothing the struggle in institutional policy and mythology, law and its collateral institutions complete the web of control over persons, benevolently dictating how to turn over fears to the state, how to turn over responsibility to the state, how to turn over consciousness, mutual aid, and sociality to the state.

But consciousness is filled not with evil but with contradictions that are resolved humanly only through a community of believers and their experiences. Only through such a collective resolution of struggle can we apprehend reality as it fully and really is.[8] And by such a commitment to community, rather than to legal and institutional abstractions, there is a commitment to one's total environment, for we begin to see ourselves as part of the universe. Alan Watts:

"we are beginning to evolve a new image of man, not as a spirit imprisoned in compatible flesh, but as an organism inseparable from his social and natural environment."[9]

Far from being the "necessary evils" of the social contract writers, the state and law, as elements external to human experience, are *unnecessary* evils. We agree with the social contract writers that only the individual is existentially real. But to promote the state, law, society or history as an existentially real entity is at the same time to deny the sanctity of the individual, to lose concern for liberty, and to create institutions that reflect little concern for individual freedom and equality.

"If government is an evil, then the laws promulgated by all governments are not only coercive restrictions on individual liberty but an intolerable form of coercion."[10] These institutions dictate the degree of value of the material world, the extent to which persons can choose to share in the world and the repertoire of myths that must be learned and pledged allegiance to. So it is that the modern state, in its democratic, fascist, welfare or administrative forms, issues forth its own typical form of coercion. Each represents or reflects the power of a megamachine that moves to be self-sufficient, "to draw into its own structure, organizations and institutions that would otherwise divert the energy it commands or divide loyalties and thus curb its automatic expansion."[11]

LEGAL DRAMA

And so it is that each state's lawyers, controllers of myth, like Wizards of Oz from behind a curtain, speak and write myths legitimizing the justness of each different form of coercion. Tolstoy:

> "the changed form and substance of law is rather like what a jailer might do who shifted a prisoner's chains from the neck to the arms, and from the arms to the legs, or took them off and substituted bolts and bars."[12]

To Tolstoy it was evident that the fundamental cause of the slavery of each historical period was legislation, the fact that there were people who had the power to create (law) myth, to transcend those myths and then build and create new mythical worlds to deal with dissenters or disbelievers. We now know that constitutions and other myths of popular law-making are lies. Laws are made by those who have institutional power. "Everywhere and always, the laws are enforced by the only means that has compelled, and still compels . . . by deprivation of liberty, and by murder."[13] Legislative processes are pure myth. "Laws are rules made by people who govern by means of organized violence, for non-compliance with which the non-complier is subjected to . . . loss of liberty, or even to being murdered."[14]

The Judiciary

The judiciary is an integral part of the enslavement drama and requires some attention. With its black robes (priests of the state), enforced deference, demanded linguistic superiority and unintelligible jargon, the judiciary cloaks the bases of law, the realities of equity, in myths of fairness. The show never stops. The armor of mystification creates and supports the values of hierarchy and authority and the interests of rulers.

The very processes of law are designed such that the

processed person is ignorant of the process, required to have others act on his behalf and to speak for him in language that is incomprehensible. The processes of law are carried out in a series of legal, psychological, medical and sociological invasions of the person. The processes of law reduce humanity, objectify persons as cases to be disposed of, sold to the highest bidder of diversion or penal program. What human alienation might have existed, the legal process completes and perfects, destroying belief in the possibility of self.

The judicial processes provide a clear example of a person's loss of language, loss of voice to speak before the community about his experiences, whatever their nature. When addressing the question of harms, personal expression is an unpermitted world. When people lose their language, they lose power over their persons, for they lose power over the realities the language represents. Throughout the legal and judicial processes some language is never allowed, taught or transmitted, as if certain words and concepts did not exist, as if certain realities did not exist, as if certain realities were not possible, as if those before the bench were personally nonexistent.

As with all criminal processes, the legislative and judicial are each their own cul-de-sac, caves of dramatic illusion in which hired actors speak as if the shadows and darkness were the only reality, as if exposure to the light's movements would be irrevocably blinding. As hired actors, professionals and experts take over the lives of those they are to help, bedecked in the arrayment of ideologies that allow them to withdraw from facing fundamental human dilemmas. As Eiseley says: "the more man thought he could withdraw from or recast nature, the more he thought that by drastic retreat he could dispel his deepening sickness."[15]

Apologists for these criminal processes, reformers and other statists, present defenses for the necessity and continuation of law, "the rule of law". In their mythical search for organizational perfection rather than in a belief in the fallibility of human experience, they state that the rule of law is better than the rule of man. This is tantamount to perfecting the shadows of reality rather than encouraging human experience to flow freely. In their reifications, they hide the fact that law is one instrument by which men have attempted to resolve the question of authority. They hide the fact that the rule of law is rule by men through violence, through isolation, punishment and coercion.[16]

Defenders of law reiterate that law and due process procedures are important means in seeking redresses of individual grievances, of inequity, injustice and abuse. They do not, however, analyze the roots of grievances, inequity, injustice and abuse and the reasons we have become a suing society. To believe that justice can be culled from bureaucratic, red tape processes in which the actors themselves have no human stake in the processes is to believe in slavery, is to defend the sources of injustice, is to promote the continuation of the American plantation.

Roots of Slavery

It becomes "evident that the essence of slavery lies not in those roots of legislation on which it now rests, but in the fact that legislation exists; that there are people who have the power to decree laws profitable for themselves, and that as long as people have that power, there will be the slavery of today and that form yet to be tried."[17] People formerly established laws enabling some people to buy and sell other people, to own them, and to make them work (slavery).[18] Today, people have established laws which consider the labor of some persons to be owned by others (capitalism). At the same time, others have established laws enabling the state to own all labor, property and persons, coercing each under pain of imprisonment, death or the declaration of being mentally unfit to work and unfit to be a part of the state.

For many, the terminology of the enslavement drama is a difficult one to accept, for it means the additional acceptance of oneself as slave while we all wish to believe ourselves free. But consider this drama within our present time. For example, some say the law defends equally the rights and property of the capitalist, landlord and worker. And yet we know that the legal "equality of the capitalist and of the worker is like the equality of two fighters when one has his arms tied and the other has weapons, but during the fight certain rules are applied to both with strict impartiality."[19]

Contradictions

We know that law is based on organized violence, created by the powerful as an instrument for historically specific enslavement. And we know that in its processes law presents an internal symbolic contradiction.[20] It pretends to distribute justice or the symbols of justice and equity, while maintaining an unjust and inequitable social order.

Defenders of law and of due process procedures argue that these institutions constrain and protect us from those involved in the "administration of justice" – the police, prosecutors, defense attorneys, juries, judges and jailors. They argue that checks on the abuses of the state's right arm can be made by twisting the state's left arm. For them, specialization, education, professionalization, pride and interaction will constrain each arm of the state. But these checks are only symbolic gestures to help perfect actors in a drama in which the actors are already dead. Such persons fail to realize that each of these sets of actors is the stomping feet of the state, that professionalization is secretization and the manufacture of mystique, that all state actors by upholding their superiority over those they process are enshrining the values of authority and hierarchy. Professionalization has led to little but standardizing and straitjacketing human activity, and to sacrificing the subjective for the objective, human expression for the maintenance of contrived, market-based identities.

The counter argument is made, however, by the defenders of law and due process, that these institutions or instruments generate principles of fairness, an increase in individual rights and the impetus to repeal unjust laws. They fail to recognize that, within the context of bureaucratic procedures and gobbledygook, due process is a way by which the state remains immune and isolated from human confrontation. Those who are professionals lose in their own lives the very human qualities they herald as their objectives. They become unfit personally by the very process in which they claim to make others "fit." Willingly or by default, they become relegated to positions as guardians of organizational ritual that ironically enhance their own peril.

The defenders of due process fail to recognize the fact that no increase in individual rights would be necessary but for the decrease created by and maintained for law. If law permitted the human community to be human, there would be no need to foster or create such concepts as due process. Indeed, there would be no need for law itself as an institution. It is to the benefit of law as an institution to maintain and promote procedural fairness, for by it its own future is insured.

At the same time, procedural defenders fail to recognize that the political economy supported by law is unjust and thus all law unjust. They fail to see that the declaration that one law is unjust (via repeal) is an illusory event. Repeal (as appeal) and similar processes are rituals to maintain and bolster the democratic myth, which says that law can be changed by "public opinion," when in fact the state and the political-economic elite allow only non-critical laws to be repealable.

In a similar vein, the defenders of law and due process procedures argue that the administration of justice requires extensive education and training for effecting justice with principle. They argue that this training subverts despotic law, mitigates cruel punishment and mercifies raw power. If this is the case, the product of training is cunning, for in actuality the trainees deliver the symbols required for the maintenance of the interests of the powerful. They deliver symbolic cases demonstrating the "humanity" of the court and its personnel; justice is served, the system, as is, works. Basic values and beliefs are unquestionable.

With this training comes professionalization, the everyday automated disposition of those in the court's clutches. Ideological training, so glorified, establishes processes that exclude all direct human response to human values and motivation, to diverse lifestyles, to multiple social realities. To behave in accordance with these exclusions would require modification of the system's ideology, also of its response to those very people it processes.

For the worker, legal education and training becomes in reality a warning not to upset the reality he sees, no matter how inhumane, and to dissolve the tensions of dissonance, not in continual reality testing and questioning of the symbols he sees, but in the appropriate use of power and organizational stratagems that will insure his survival. In short, training becomes the official initiating act in the creation of an organizationally docile human animal. The trainee learns to decode the organizational (hierarchical) violence he sees in terms of valid administrative practice and to forfeit any human considerations for the status of organization man, citizen. He learns not to "fight the system" and in doing so begins to lean over to die. Mumford:

> "The business of creating a limited, docile, scientifically conditioned human animal, completely adjusted to a purely technological environment, has kept pace with the rapid transformation of that environment itself: partly this has been effected, as already noted, by re-enforcing conformity with tangible rewards, partly by denying any real opportunities for choices outside the range of the megatechnic system."[21]

The defenders of law and due process procedures argue that law in the modern state could not be a simple reflection of economic relationships, or too blatantly an instrument of the ruling class. Engels argued that "as a legal system is elaborated, it develops a life and logic of its own, and is constrained by the demands of internal consistency. A legal system has, therefore, an internal dynamic towards the realization of principles of equity and justice embodied within a legal code."[22]

Can it be that law is a subversive process or, as Engels argues, that legal processes yield their antithesis? Is the process of law in everyday affairs, in the invasion of our lives, actually busy destroying the injustices of its political-economic base? When and if law does destroy law, will it not surely become an unfit instrument for those in power?

Possibly these contradictions hold some validity. Possibly, a familiarity with law and its processes can heighten or intensify a consciousness of social injustice. However, it is certain that those subject to legal and penal processes are not first acquainted with injustice in the court, police station, prison or jail.

There are, in fact, signs that law is becoming subversive of the power it serves and is being replaced as the major instrument of state control by a more effective institution. The welfare state with its host of activities tends "to coordinate new policing functions and to bolster more traditional sources of 'law and order'."[23] As instruments of control, administrative rules and bureaucracy are far more subtle forms of incursion and control and far more congruent with the needs of technology, which requires control of persons at every possible juncture.

So, as we come to the point of a post-scarcity society, to a society of abundance, administrative rules and bureaucracy become highly critical, for they serve to maintain a steady and compliant clientele. When people agreed on scarcity, they also agreed on accepting the legal mandates to behave in certain ways to insure food and services. They were even willing to accept the negative consequences of consumption and natural destruction. We have come to the point now, however, where the gratifications technology offers us no longer bind us together. Many are not willing to consume when it means a war economy which must destroy nature and people. As these individuals become more vocal, the administrative rules become ever more sophisticated for controlling them. Moreover, administrative rules begin to be talked about and used as moral codes when in fact they were once only successful managerial stratagems. The classical ideologies of law are slowly being displaced by the ideologies of science.

SCIENCE IS A FUNCTIONAL EQUIVALENT OF LAW

Within the ideology of science, each person is no longer conceived of as rational, equally human or voluntaristic. She or he is no longer seen as capable of directly resolving his or her conflicts with equals with whom she or he must live the next day. She or he is no longer conceived of as in need of protection from the state. No longer is the reaction of state functionaries to be neither arbitrary, nor an incursion of individual sanctity. No longer is their response to entail a symbolic response to the act, meaning to deter others from similar acts; and no longer is the act offensive, for the part is seen and taken as the whole. The act is now equated with the essence of the actor.

According to the ideology of science, each person is determined by forces of which she or he is unaware. As a consequence, she or he is not responsible for his or her actions. She or he does not make choices but is acted upon. The offensive act signifies (is a symptom) that the actor is sick, imbalanced, unsocialized or chromosomically deviant. The actor is a "criminal." His or her whole being is criminal. She or he is different from us and unequal, essentially a part of another world that itself needs reordering.

Conflicts must be resolved scientifically by experts, not juridical ones, but those superior unequals who, from their privileged view of the world, understand the malaise of the "criminal." They can treat the criminal into compliance, into leaving the world of destructive infatuation, and into obedience. They can treat the criminal through castration, lobotomization, electrocution or total elimination. No longer does she or he need protection from the state, for she or he is the state. All is the state, sorting out eugenically its own worst breeding.

The law is not an instrument of science. Under the more sophisticated ideology of scientific control, law becomes cumbersome, old-fashioned and obsolete. It is no longer required.

It does not provide the necessary cover for the complex welfare state. The "criminal" needs to be re-educated, to be bureaucratically processed, medically or scientifically judged different. She or he needs to be contained until she or he thinks, feels and acts "correctly."

Aspects of both the ideology of law and the ideology of science are, however, reflected in our current state criminal control apparatus. Though science and law are conflicting ideologies, especially regarding the issues of responsibility, volition and state benevolence, they are equally serviceable to those in power. Both focus on the individual through symbolic deterrent processing or treatment. Both uphold the superiority of the experts, judicial or scientific, and both postulate a one-reality consensual view of the world. They thrive on the unchallenged consensus that all believe in the morality and permanence of the present distributions of power, property, knowledge, life chance and liberty. Neither questions the current political-economic-social order. Rather, both owe their presence and allegiance to serve to maintain this present order. (Note: We are trying to point out the common assumptions of the ideologies, not to posit a consensus among either scientists or lawyers or between them. Some lawyers and some scientists may reject these ideas.)

The "administration of justice" in the modern state is thus a cunning, if confusing, mix of these ideologies. Modern state law is not a simple reflection of economic, monopolist interests and ruling class values. It is a carefully constructed mix of custom, morality, status politics among moral entrepreneurs, and ruling class interests. Kropotkin[24] argues that this cunning recipe involves: protection of the unjust appropriation of others' labor; lubrication for the machinery of government by which this theft is protected; the sweetener of social custom; and the inert "claim of protection of the person." This legal mix must then be spiced with the fads of the time to make it interesting and marketable. It can then be poured into any form, for neither its size nor its shape are critical. And, from this, we are made to consume a slippery, sweet, deceivingly protective food. And while we pay for the ingredients, and supply the labor, it closes our eyes, warps our minds, and nourishes the ruling few.

LEGAL PROBLEMATICS

What is more, the sweet substance of law is baked to resolve all problems. Laws are so numerous that no one could possibly not break them. There are laws that individuals choose to break and laws which individuals are forced to break. The scope and invasive depth of law has reached totalistic proportions. The whole of society has come to take on the properties of a "total institution," best characterized as an asylum. The state has become the "protector," the "parent," the "teacher," the "punisher" and the "murderer" of the individual. The individual has become the property, the tool, the inert extension of the machine of the state.

The state has become the national megamachine, and as the chief protagonist of the war has usurped authority over all components of our civilization: geographical, biological and anthropological. "Indeed the most frenetic advocates of this process are proclaiming that the whole biological world is now being supplanted by technology, and that man will either become a willing creature of his technology or cease to exist."[25]

Permeation, Proliferation, Discretion

The totalistic monopolization of the individual via law allows state enforcers to exercise discretion against those persons whom they desire to control. If all laws were strictly enforced, everybody would be criminalized; the full meaning and impact of law would become too directly felt. Discretion allows the police to close their eyes to certain acts and actors, but also allows them to conceive of themselves as the law, "the man." It allows the judge to interpret the "spirit of the law," to excuse, to determine responsibility, and to state: "In my court, what I say the law is, is the law." The judge becomes the paid and spurious prophet of a community that

58

does not exist and that does not have the creative tensions to accept prophecy. The proliferation of law and its component, discretion, produces and reinforces attitudes of superiority and authority and blinds the eyes of the community to their own creative experiences. Discriminatory discretion piles injustice on injustice. Those selected for control, for symbolic processing, are nevertheless those most unjustly situated in the political economy.

All eyes are closed to those of the propertied, ruling few. Their activities are subject to "civil law" if at all. Civil law becomes the ritualistic duel of swords of the nobility where a truce is struck as the first blood of the opponent is drawn, when the symbolic reality of the system is satisfied. When subjected to criminal law, the ruling caste purchases shrewd lawyers, stocks the jury, bribes the judge, is declared "rehabilitated the instant they are arrested" or have their actions cleansed of responsibility through the legal categories of corporation or trust. When criminal law enters the caste's theatre the duel turns to full-fledged battle, the rich arm. Unlike the rich, "there is only one law for the poor, to wit: obey the rich."[26]

From an elitist point of view, it would seem strategic to allow law to seep into all realms of individual activity. It would seem strategic to allow people to urge the law and law enforcement to act on anything which seems immoral and unacceptable to them. Moreover, it would seem that a public passion for morality would protect and shield law and law enforcement agents far more efficiently than the state could alone.[27] Such support for law enforcement has created a climate tolerant of police violence, the infiltration of political and dissident groups, the development of police power and the increasing centralization of violent force. But, ironically, discretion and the proliferation of law have created problems of legitimacy for the law; that is, support for the expansion of criminal law and increased interference with individual liberty have created a climate destructive of legal legitimacy.

Defenders of the present legal-political-economic order

have amassed a great amount of evidence indicating that the extension of criminal law into the private sphere has been harmful and ineffective.[28] The extension of law, for example, into "crimes without victims or complainants", proactive law enforcement (i.e. "stop and frisk") and direct political action, have eroded law enforcement and legal authority. Electronic surveillance, informers, decoys, agents provocateurs, hired "yippies", plumbers, media setups and other methods of questionable legality and unquestionable unacceptability erode the legitimacy of law and the state. Responding to these issues within the framework of legality, experts have argued for a shrinkage of the extension of law and law enforcement from private and consenting realms. They argue for this de-criminalization on the basis that the fiscal and temporal costs involved divert resources and make ineffective attempts to control serious street crime. They also argue for decriminalization on the basis that principles are eroded, that the means delegitimate the ends. They argue that new ways must be found to manage and control people, even if "non-intervention" is the most effective program.[29]

Somewhere in the minds of these experts must be implanted the dream that through some mystical asymmetry, non-response on the part of the state will induce obedience and conformity, as if not paying attention to relationship might provide the milieu in which community might emerge. They write, if not to explicitly preserve the legitimacy of the current social order, then at least as though its goodness, since unmentioned, were beyond question. Behind the curtain of law they speak like Oz of non-intervention and de-criminalization when the state, the entire world, is being centralized! To respond within the frame of legality does no justice to the sanctity of person or community.

Obscurity and Unintelligibility

Discretion, legal proliferation and increasing state permeation are not, however, the only legal problematics. The obscurity of law and the language of law, which has become unintelligible to nearly everyone, including lawyers, are equally oppressive. The obscurity of the law diminishes individual responsibility for legal conformity. The individual is uninformed as to what is proscribed. There is neither clarity nor certainty of state response. At the same time, the law's linguistic unintelligibility continues to render it both private and particular.[30]

These characteristics of law have several significant effects. For one, lawmakers, along with scientists, claim the exclusive cognitive ability to resolve the problem of social control and all the other problems of life. This serves to reinforce the values and practices of hierarchy and authority. It encourages people to feel incapable of resolving their own problems, leaving them dependent and non-responsible for the conditions they live under. Furthermore, it fosters feelings of inferiority and renders people inert and submissive, and suppresses the consciousness that *they are history* and the creators of their own destiny and identity. Of immediate consequence is a consciousness that imprisons, in such a way that people seek surrogates for face-to-face relationships, refusing the experiences of relationship and interdependence. That each is holy and capable of community, that is, sacred and giving primacy to life, is regarded as mythical.

A second effect of the obscurity and linguistic mask of law is that legal interpretation is relegated to an elite few. This fact greases the wheels of selective enforcement, selective prosecution, selective rulings, selective interpretations and selective processing. It also makes law school popular as a perceived expressway to mobility, for as long as law is a prime instrument of protection for the ruling few, the ability to write, manipulate, skirt and find loopholes in the law will be in great demand. The skills of the cunning and shrewd legal mind are highly saleable to those private interests who can retain them. From generation to generation, the legal profession plays a major part in institutionalizing the positions of the elite in their survival-of-the-fittest design, passing on the social-economic-political genes that insure dominance and destruction. The legal profession becomes an institution in the subtle catharsis of benign neglect and the social eugenics of capitalistic societies.

THE IRONIES OF SERVING POWER

While there are personal "advantages" heralded as reasons for participating in the legal drama, those who file for positions as legal instruments soon discover *themselves* as objects, as persons to be used. They soon find themselves in the midst of processes which no one seems to have directly created. They become chained to file drawers, to libraries, to paper they find meaningless for life processes. They have little control over the types of cases or issues on which they work. They find their ideas, briefs and arguments destructively altered or used in ways that offend their sense of morality and justice. The lawyer is reduced to impotence and lifeless motions in the script of the power drama and its rituals. Some, however, realize their paralysis and begin to act to utilize their skills differently. They refuse to be manipulated any longer and desire to become quite differently involved in social life. The legal practice in defense of the powerful is, however, insured as it is bureaucratized, controlled and specialized. Such disengagement and conflict resolution is accommodated, assured, and institutionalized.

Power, bureaucratic and legal, destructively forces all aspects of life into the straitjacket of universal consensual reality. Its intellectual form is dead dogma (law), while its physical form is brute force. The objectives of power, controlling the liberty of others, set a stamp on its supporters, rendering them "stupid and brutal, even when they were originally endowed with the best of talents. One who is constantly striving to force everything into a hierarchical mechanical order at last becomes a machine himself and loses all human feeling."[31] And yet these very processes of serving power may take on a liberative dimension – as people begin to free themselves from and subvert the power machine, unmasking the power system for what it is, disclosing the robber in the act, liberating the server from the career of chains.

These dialectical processes apply to all power servers whose activities fall within the domain of destruction: non-domestic "administrators of justice" – soldiers, military bureaucrats, diplomats, attachés, advisors, agents provocateurs, missionaries, "foreign servicers," and "peace" corps type personnel; and welfare-state servers – policemen, lawyers, judges, prosecutors, jailers, guards, social workers, scientists and teachers. All must begin to come to grips with the meaning of their social role and conscience, for they are all chained to the power structure as servants, in turn chaining others.

Policemen, for example, faced with the direct task of the power structure's dirty work, reap tremendous marital and relational problems and leave their jobs at an astounding rate. If they remain they either turn "soft", adopting a non-enforcement, aiding orientation to the problems with which people face them, or become brutal, calloused, racist, indifferent, and dehumanized from those whom they police, from themselves, their children, from all of us.[32] Within the confines of both forms of adaptations to hierarchy, they share in the destruction the law enforcement agency has as its mission. They are its fettered instruments, unable while they remain within its web to transcend the requirements of slavery.

In a similar way, guards, as Kropotkin and Berkman experienced,[33] are as brutalized by prison as are prisoners. If they remain guards, they become petty, filled with intrigue, sadistic, ritualistic, totalitarian, chained by the very bars and keys they use to close on others. They become so dehumanized that they themselves become objects of their own oppressive acts and thoughts. Confirming this, Zimbardo in his dramatic Stanford Prison Experiment demonstrated that "normal" students in becoming "guards" rapidly dehumanized themselves by the way they treated "experimental" prisoners. Everyone involved found the culture of imprisonment to be devastating and brutal. Zimbardo himself, upon the realization that he had become a warden, became extremely remorseful.[34]

Many teachers also face social imprisonization as they constantly strive to force students to learn programmed facts, to absorb canned knowledge, and to reason with the one correct "logic." In the lecture hall, on television, or via machine, the student becomes a numbered object, a nameless entity and the price paid for continuing in the processes of state/ professional certification is one's humanity. Teachers and students alike become humanly worthless, inaccessible, unapproachable, and undisclosing of their own person. The education process is regularly segregated from each person's reality; it is abstract, and, by its form and brand of coercion, unappreciative of the life and liberty of its participants.

Scientists are similarly enmeshed in the imprisonization process. The scientist, vain in his or her intellect and base in his or her power over "things" (chemicals, rocks) and other "forms of life" (plants, flowers, rats, primates), finds welcome expansion in performing the same experiments on humans. Be the experiments drug-induced identity conversions, chemical or germ warfare exterminations, token economies, electro- or chemo-surgeries, floating missile technologies or welfare-income-housing project policies, all are designed to regulate and control other persons. In this the scientist discovers his or her handmaiden's role. She or he is subordinate, an instrument of the ruling elite. She or he does not have the power to protect him- or herself from becoming an object, from experimentation.[35] She or he learns, ironically, that knowledge is neither value-free nor neutral, but is rather an expression of person which is the essence of value. She or he learns that access to knowledge and the opportunity to use knowledge are differentially distributed, skewed in the direction of those with power.

What a person does to engage in such activities cannot be regarded as neutral or value-free or as having no relationship to what the hiring organization does. If you seek positions of power, to be a decision-maker, to make a career out of directing others, you are part of the corruption of the state and share in its oppression. To make a life activity of exercising power is to perpetuate a malevolent state of human affairs. It is to partake in the genetic transfer of elitist, ruling class

64

characteristics. For in power organizations you must continue to prove your potency, superiority and power or you will panic for fear of being victimized yourself, for fear of losing your identity or of being devoured.[36] But if you continue, you will increasingly de-energize yourself. Mutual aid, initiative and life decisions will be further monopolized by the powerful. Goodman:

> "As people become stupider and more careless, administration increases in size and power; and conversely."[37]

If you seek positions of power, decision-making for others, you become criminal. Inspecting, bossing, registering, classifying, evaluating, ordering, rehabilitating, paroling, executing, spying, or informing places one firmly within the pattern of power holder.[38] "He who attempts to control another is a governor, an aggressor, an invader; and the nature of such invasion is not changed, whether it is made by one man upon another man, after the manner of the ordinary criminal, or by one man upon all others, after the manner of an absolute monarch, or by all other men upon one man, after the manner of a modern democracy."[39] The harms of power-server, "criminal," and "governor" have a common denominator. (Note: We do not mean to suggest that those acts which states define as crime are *per se* harmful or morally wrong. For example it might be illegal but it is neither harmful nor wrong for a black person to freely travel throughout a South African city.) All are the invasions of individual or personal liberty. Yet the harms of the state and the harms of penal sanction are far greater than those of ordinary offenses. The suffering, dehumanization, psychological and moral harm of prison far outweigh the harm of ordinary offenses. The suffering, displacement, burns, deaths and bloodbath of war by far displace the blood of all "crime" in the streets. The misery, hunger, colonization and resource extraction of capitalism far surpass the harms of common theft. That the former are intentionally clothed in myth aggravates the harm of the acts themselves.

SOCIAL ORGANIZATION AND RESPONSIBILITY

Becoming a power server or governor lulls us into an adaptation in which we lose our sense of personal responsibility, both for ourselves and for others. It is an adaptation of self-interest and self-loss, causing us to live with and next to one another without knowing, understanding or appreciating one another. It leads us to become unconcerned, uncommitted, unaiding of others, which at some point turns into a calculated defensiveness and insensitivity. A starving child, a starving population, a victim of street violence, a victim of state violence is not our direct concern or responsibility. "Others" will act, charities will feed the hungry, police will aid the street crime victim, the state will control the violence of the state. And "so the state is justified for solving the problems it creates!"[40]

As soon as a person enters into the power drama, personal energies are directed to survival and exploitation. Therefore, a kind of survival of the fittest philosophy is espoused that permits the conscience to watch others (segments of the population) be destroyed and disappear. Better them than me! As each nation-state practices triage on an international level, each welfare state practises the same principle within its bounds, as if all could not live and be free. Never is the connection between the hunger for power and the demise of people discussed in the education system or the courts, for these and other welfare-state institutions pile unconnected world upon unconnected world with a mythology the components of which are well connected and closely interwoven.

If you seek positions of power, decision-making for others, you enter and become part of the rationalized, centralized state that seeks divisiveness. You become part of the segmenting processes that allow the healing state to continue through its triage. But within the state you will find that no one is responsible for anything. Neither Nixon nor Calley nor Lodge, nor anyone in between. Neither Hitler nor Dachau executioner nor Churchill, nor anyone in between.

66

In the "administration of criminal justice", a euphemism for the welfare state's triage process, neither policeman, nor judge, nor social worker, nor warden accepts responsibility. The system's division of labor designates each party responsible for only part of the process, for part of the segmented world. As it makes each processor responsible for only one part of the processed person, it also divides the processor into triplicate. People are as whole as the kind of work they do. Consciousness is work activity. In a paper world the paper self is never whole, the real self is never met for it is never whole. Such insulation from the responsibility for one's actions! While the division of labor we are talking about provides protection for one's accrual of power through its insulating mechanisms, it does not protect the person from the far more serious threat that one will never be whole or even come to grips with one's humanity.

This division of labor separates the policy maker from the policy implementors. Responsibility is vacated. It escapes through a gap in the chain of hierarchy. If the policy is hailed a success, the maker accepts accolades. If designated a failure, the policy was misinterpreted, mismanaged, sabotaged by the implementors. Responsibility dissolves in the rhetoric of survival. At any rate, the persons involved are further removed from the activities they supposedly direct, further removed from the earth and its touch.

Such a division of labor in the modern state and bureaucracies also makes individual policy rare. The policy maker is a group, not a person. The jury, the supreme court, the diagnostic center, the congress, the party, the committee, the corporation, these policy makers are not persons. Responsibility cannot be taken by a group. The group has no existential reality and thus cannot be responsible. A corporation cannot be imprisoned for polluting rivers and lakes. Legal or social creations of collective actors are devices for the evasion of responsibility and the acquisition of power. The sacred and secret jury, the committee, corporation and legislature are creations cloaking the manipulation of life by those in power. Bureaucracies, committees, "administrations" have no mor-

67

ality, have no principles!

As we understand division of labor in the hierarchical sense, it is a work form in which it is envisaged that the rationality, productivity and profit of a task is enhanced. A division of labor is a form of cooperation pursued with the intent that work will be lessened, freeing individuals to pursue activities of their own choosing. But it is a form of cooperation which is not frequently direct, not frequently joyful, not frequently artistic.

In fact we see the division of labor in hierarchical organizations negating freedom, never facilitating the freeing of the ghosts within. As long as the freedom from work is owned by the few and the nature of the tasks defined by the few, little of the advantage of the division of labor accrues to the laborers. For the owners of labor, it becomes profitable to automate the tasks and to not employ additional sets of workers. As calves are killed to maintain the profit margin on beef, though there are persons starving daily in the United States, so also people are laid off to maintain other corporate profit margins. As "the market" changes, it becomes profitable to increase production or specialization or unemployment rates such that work becomes more alienating or non-obtainable. Commitment to work, pride, is lost, as is one's talent, individuality and self. And the more the processing of people is "rationalized" as a productive endeavor, the more it requires individuals to continuously perform a specific task, the more it delineates codes to tell them when they are to perform the tasks, how they are to perform them (speed, order, method), and where they are to perform them, the more each worker loses his or her freedom. Though the specified division of labor might satisfy the organizer's judgement of quality or function, that it is superimposed on the work experience makes for increasing dissatisfaction and erodes the possibility of worker judgement. Whether the organizers are processing objects through the organization of labor (capitalism) or processing persons through the organization of power (government), liberty is reduced, the possibility of freedom negated.

The more the judgment of workers becomes rational and controlled, the more they themselves become objects, economies of scale, resources to be manipulated. Life choices come to be understood only within the context of the objective realities of bosses. Under the guise of rationality, life choices are narrowed, the worker becomes an object, means, statistic, opinion, body, resource and instrument to be maneuvered by political rulers, by the few the law concedes subjective reality to and then protects. For law protects the entire set of processes and objectification ceremonies we are talking about.

As forced labor and specialization are substitutes for talent and collective commitment, legal "prohibition is a substitute for direct participation."[41] Neither those who control nor those who are controlled ever come close to experiencing human reality. For they are engaged in the reality of oppressing and being oppressed and of jockeying for power – always at least once removed from existential experience. The means by which we attempt to obtain our ends soon themselves become our end.[42] Power becomes the "be-all" and "end-all" of living. Economic division sets person against person; political division sets people against people; hierarchical division bolsters attitudes of superiority, authority, racism, nationalism and any attitude that the division requires as its character undergoes historical change.

In the life of hierarchy, control by the few, centralization, there is war within and war without. The few must be armed and ceaselessly on guard. Through breathing oppression and deceit, they are bound to regard all, within and outside their domain, as enemies. They are forced to be in a state of continuous conspiracy against all.[43]

The history of Western civilization has been one continuous Ides of March. Christians, intent upon their own salvation, withdrew from too great an intimacy with the natural. They drove the natural deities from the hillsides and trees, drove pagan images from the minds and souls of men. From then on "becoming civilized" meant the elimination from consciousness of one deity after another whereby "man no longer saw distinct and powerful spirits in every tree or running brook."[44] There was no longer sanctity in nature.

With science the process becomes more sophisticated, the destruction more subtle. With the megamachine and automated division of labor, man begins to destroy these godless hillsides and trees; himself now subject to the same destruction he had invoked in the machine. Eiseley:

"He, too, in a new fashion, would be relegated soulless to the wood with all his lurking irrationalities exposed."[45]

Like Polyphemus, man had become the monster controlling the avenues to freedom as "One eye, one bulging eye, the technological, scientific eye, was willing to count man as well as nature's creatures in terms of megadeaths. Its objectivity had become so great as to endanger its master, who was mining his own brains as ruthlessly as a seam of coal."[46] All within the bounds of law, Western civilization epitomized by the United States has been reduced to shock status, where the choice has come to: either the life of an abstract ideological system or the life of the species.

Still all sorts of dramatic scripts are played out *as if* nothing had happened that reduces persons to shock status. If the surface institution of law is scratched by disclosures of illegalities (assassinations, Watergates, secret subversion funds, illegal surveillance, etc.) polish is applied. New laws, new elections (France, 1968), new presidents (United States, 1974), new detente, new contracts are contrived to serve the times.

Direct violent actions remain a last resort, for once the velvet glove has been put on the iron fist, it is politically very risky to take it off. When the velvet is worn, it is quickly patched by the smoothening effect of media, senate hearings, blue ribbon panels, authoritarian opposition parties (a traditional Communist Party role), labor leadership or more law, more velvet. The law, the state, the bureaucracy guard the fist of capital; they are the velveteen police.

In modern party dictatorship states, the velvet is in the skin. The fist, the flesh and glove are inseparable. The police, bureaucracy, law and capitalist are one. The power of the fist is quite exposed. The iron law of oligarchy, the rule of the few, the iron law of decadence, the creation of secrecy, and the privatization of law are quite uncovered. The oppression and surveillance of the velveteen police is strengthened and the ruling clique retains its franchise of power. All is police as the thread of surveillance winds its way through the entire fabric of the social garment. All is force as the threat of reprisal for anything said or felt is omnipresent. Henry Adams predicted this as early as 1905:

> "The assumption of unity, which was the mark of human thought in the Middle Ages, has yielded slowly to the proofs of complexity. The stupor of science before radium is proof of it. Yet it is quite sure, according to my score of ratios and curves, that, at the accelerated rate of progression since 1600, it will not need another century or half century to turn thought upside down. Law in that case would disappear as theory or *a priori* principle and give place to force. Morality would become police. Explosives would reach cosmic violence. Disintegration would overcome integration."[47]

The irreversible changes of industrial society and the demand the legal system would make for internal consistency, even if it meant sacrificing the humanity that gave it presence, demand that law, police and the state, whatever their form, must be abolished. They must be abolished in ways that do *not* contain forms of hierarchy and authority that exist outside the experiences in question. This means the rejection of central committees for these only create new modes of law, police and state and should be rejected as readily as the violence in current forms of hierarchy. With hierarchy and centralization in any form, experience is secondary to social order. Whatever their nuances, these organizational modes deny to the individual liberty and morality; for "the moment that orders, enforced by legal penalties, replace the personal impulses of the conscience" morality is denied.[48]

LIBERTY AND JUSTICE FOR ALL

Liberty is not to be found in legal rights, constitutions or laws. Nor is it to be found in being freed from these institutions. "Real freedom, true liberty, is positive: it is freedom to something; it is the liberty to be, to do; in short, the liberty of actual and active opportunity."[49] It is not an egoistic opting out of a society or an escape from self. It is an active participation in "a society in which all the mutual relations of its members are regulated, not by laws, not by authorities, whether self-imposed or elected, but by mutual agreements between the members of the society, and by a sum of social customs and habits – not petrified by law, routine or superstition, but continually developing and continually readjusted, in accordance with the ever-growing requirements of a free life, stimulated by the progress of science, invention and the steady growth of higher ideals."[50]

For freedom is "a state of being in which man's relatedness to life is unobstructed. Unobstructed either by concepts or by fear or by ignorance or by deformity. Freedom permits us to live into experience within and without."[51] It means being sensitive to the rhythms of nature and seasons, to experience the natural, seeing oneself as part of the natural. Law, with its requirements of mystification, is the opposite: to accept nothing but the power arrangements of the few that enforce spurious rhythms and patterns of time, limit the possibilities of experience, turn self from self, and posit the dimensions by which we become our own slavery force, unable to free ourselves for life's journey.

No ruling authorities, then. No government of man by man. No crystalization and immobility but a continual evolution such as we see in nature. Free movement for the individual, for the full development of his or her individual gifts, for his or her individualization.[52] When individuals can choose the mode of their activity, the conditions of this activity and the freedom to this activity, they will become artists. Their work will reflect inspiration, interest, a self that is a creative force.[53]

People will become voluntarily productive, equal contractors, personalized actors and exchangers of goods. Human interaction, mutual aid, solidarity and spontaneity can be

72

realized only under such conditions of economic and social equality and the experiences that lead to such a society, not by thinking harder or more rational processes. Economic and social equality define justice. "Justice is based on the recognition that other men are equally important. Unless men have the experience of mutually helpful associations, they will develop the sense of neither equality nor justice."[54] Equality generates friendship and full regard for all and excludes the threatening insecurity of hierarchy, whatever its brand. "Benevolence degenerates into tyranny, and admiration into servility."[55] The morality evolved from equality would not distinguish what one does for oneself from what one does for others. Neither altruism nor egoism would retain a social base.[56]

The possibility exists that there is no social order which we can conceive of or bring about which will not produce genuine contradictions and social change. Perhaps social life is a permanent contradiction and there are no resolutions. Yet a life lived in economic and social equality, mutual aid and individual liberty would surely reduce the harms with which we are now familiar (rape, penal sanction, economic exploitation, war). We would meet directly and collectively the many social contradictions and conflicts we now face, as we would the realization that each of us is unique and yet possesses an equal humanness, as we would the realization that the meaning of self is separate and yet socially constructed, and as we would the dilemmas of rationality and freedom, of power and principle.

To face these "problems" of human bonding and survival directly and collectively means to restore them to a direct, face-to-face level. It means that instead of the proscribing of behaviour through law or religious ethic, or controlling behavior through science or technology, the individual will be free to develop his or her own morality. It means that instead of denying or passing off responsibility to committee or bureaucracy, the individual will act with full responsibility for his or her behavior. It means that children will develop true human dignity and self reliance because they will have aged and

73

acted with full responsibility.[57] It means that we will all be responsible to ourselves and to all others.

When social harms are considered, they are defined and recognized as having meaning for all individuals. This means that when a social harm is believed to have occurred, each individual must re-evaluate his/her responsibilities to the community. It means, in a very real sense, that there is an ethic of shared responsibility. There is a collective or extended responsibility for the acts of each, the sense being that the circumstances had not heretofore been fully explored, emotions not fully expressed and needs not fully met.

Direct justice means no institutionalization of the resolving of conflict. It means that there is no base on which institutions such as civil law, involving restitution, can be distinguished from punitive, penal or retributive law. It means that no distinctions can be drawn between the power to maim and the power to pardon, both falling under the same guise of destruction. Such distinctions had their derivation in hierarchical justice (restitutive law for within-class conflicts, and retributive law for between-class conflicts). With equality and without the divisiveness of law, conflicts are to be resolved through confrontation, reconsideration, and forgiveness of harms rather than through restitution or retribution. Each person is seen as part of an interacting environment and individuals must resolve their own conflicts while upholding the liberty of each. Conflicting persons must reconstruct, recontract or renegotiate their relationship.

These processes might include the airing of conflicts among mutually selected friends. Perhaps the persons in conflict could select a mediator. In any case, face-to-face justice would be different from "justice" imposed by outside legal authority having a stake in repressing the offender. Direct justice involves airing the complexities of the situation and the reality of returning to work and living with the other person.

"Justice must be warm, must be living; it cannot be shut up within the boundaries of a profession."[58] Face-to-face justice is an outgrowth of life, needing no special or permanent personages or languages, no office of authority or imposition. If individuals resolve their conflicts by no longer holding to past contracts, then so be it, as all relationships are ever renegotiable, impermanent and dependent upon voluntary commitment. Punishment, retribution, deterrence and protection are concepts logically consistent with imposed authority and loss of human dignity. They are by-words for ceremonies of enslavement in a society in which slavery is cherished. Treatment, re-education, work camps, therapy and modification are concepts logically consistent with state scientism, the updated welfare-warfare technology of bureaucratic control. They also specify imposed authority and loss of human dignity.

Liberty, liberty and more liberty are the concepts logically consistent with equality, order, justice and anarchy. Liberty is the freedom to be holy, to be sensitive to the movement and rhythms of human mystery that persist in the struggle of the individual to search for community. At the same time, it is intertwined with the belief that each of us has the power to free ourselves, that the more we rely on abstractions and organizations that do not free, the more we lose that power and, by omission, ourselves begin to lose our freedom, begin to slide into a unique form of enslavement that denies us each our journey. It is a return to a reality based in the shadows of hierarchy and submission. It is our struggle to free the ghosts within and to remain in the light outside the caves of hierarchy that brings us to collectivize. It is through shared responsibility for life that the power to be free is given impetus.

SUMMARY

Law is the inversion of person and community. Its presence signifies a diminished receptivity to personal and collective diversity. Unmasked, law is recognized as destructive of order, as protective of invasion, as based on organized violence. The slavery of each historical period has been the existence of those with the power to create legitimating myths. To accept law means to explore justice and freedom only within its mechanics. To accept law is to justify the state (no matter its form) for solving the harms and miseries it creates. To accept law means that an abused child, a starving population, a victim of street violence, and a victim of state violence are not our direct concern or responsibility. Thus, law and its supported relationships are not tolerable.

Surely the harms with which we are now too familiar (rape, industrial murder, war, penal sanction, economic exploitation, mugging) can be reduced if we reject law and construct communities in which equality, mutual aid, and individual liberty prevail. The many and necessary contradictions and conflicts can be resolved directly and collectively. Instead of denying or passing off responsibility to a committee or bureaucracy, each can act with full responsibility for all. Justice in daily life, and the ways in which we respond to grievances, conflicts and disputes can be based on the needs of the persons involved.

2   Social Harms: Crime and Penal Sanction

For a man to coerce a woman into domestic or sexual submission, for the state to pour electricity or a term of prison
confinement into that man as punishment are both social
harms, for crime and penal sanction are social harms of the
same order. Both have their origin and continuity in the presence of historically specific ideas and institutions. Both are
forms of behavior which attempt to control, invade and
destroy another human being. Crime is a specific type of
invasion, a specific type of "normative" violation. Penal sanction is, as well, a specific type of invasion, a specific type of
reprisal. To begin to think about and challenge the presence
of one kind of harm without the other is to accept the illusion
of two worlds, one of which, for the sake of its own privilege
and survival, controls the other by controlling lives which
struggle for authenticity within the concentration camp conditions of its everinvading presence. Crime and penal sanction are of the same world. (Note: In this chapter crime will
be defined in a number of different ways. At this initial point
in our analysis we wish to adopt a legal (state) definition of
crime. We will later reject this legal (state) definition and
explore the acts, harms, and invasions of economic elites and
the state itself – those who are now beyond incrimination. In
initially adopting the legal (state) definition we do not mean
to suggest that those acts which the state defines as crime are
per se either harms, invasions, or morally wrong. In fact, there
are numerous crimes that are not harms (for example loiter-
ing, being black and without proper papers in the "white"
territories of South Africa, leaving home at a youthful age,

77

and perhaps drinking alcohol). Undeniably, there are crimes that are harms (for example rape). Furthermore, there are harms that are not now defined as crimes (for example capital punishment, imprisonment, war, poisoning the earth, racism, sexism, ageism, and perhaps corporal disciplining of children).)

"Crime is here defined as a violation, by act or omission, of any criminal law. According to that law, it is also a specific conduct leading to a harm and is an act construed as a harm against a state. It follows that deviations from norms which are not criminal laws are not crimes. It also follows that in any society where such laws are absent there is no crime."

"Punishment (penal sanction) is an intended harm imposed by one or more parties upon an individual over whom those who impose that harm have assumed or have been granted jurisdiction as a right – a right contingent upon superior coercive power or collectively given power to exempt an offender from a reprisal for his offense. Penal sanction is a special case of punishment, and both are special cases of intended harms generally."[1] Acts (whether proscribed by law or not) which are not defined as harms against the state, or for which penal sanction is not prescribed, are not crimes. The decisive characteristics of criminal law are politicality (harm against the state) and penal sanction (prescribed punishment). Both characteristics presuppose a state, both presuppose criminal law. "There can be no crime in any social order which has no state."[2]

The formally rational state is a post-fifteenth century development in Western culture. Crime and penal sanction are linked to formal laws and the formal, rational state. Both crime and penal sanction emerged historically with the state, with the transformation of the ethic of shared responsibility for individual conduct to the ethic of individual responsibility.[3]

There are now, have been, and will be societies with no state. The state was invented and continues to be invented, to be maintained and re-created. The invented state was "an institution which not only secured the newly acquired riches

78

of individuals against the communistic traditions of the gentile order, which not only sanctified the private property formerly so little valued, and declared this sanctification to be the highest purpose of all human society; but an institution which set the seal of general social recognition on each new method of acquiring property and thus amassing wealth at continually increasing speed; an institution which perpetuated, not only this growing cleavage of society into classes, but also the right of the possessing class to exploit the non-possessing, and the rule of the former over the latter."[4] The state emerged to protect and promote the interests of the newly emerging propertied, merchant class. One instrument for this protection was law, the monopolization of force, embodied in codes as the means of enforcing these interests.[5] "In the early states, crimes were invented to serve the needs of the state; that is, legal sanctions were needed to protect the new interests of the emerging state. Rather than healing any breaches of custom, law protected the sovereign. The state necessarily broke up customary patterns in the interest of economic and political dominance, and instituted a legal system to enforce its sovereignty".[6] Law arose in the breach of a prior customary order and increased in force with the conflict that divided political societies internally and among themselves. "Law and order is the historical illusion; law versus order is the historical reality."[7]

THE HISTORICAL EMERGENCE OF CRIME AND PENAL SANCTION

To better understand the historical emergence of crime and penal sanction we must explain the order out of which individual incrimination, law and the state arose.

In the first feudal age neither criminal law, penal sanction, nor the institution of capitalism had emerged. No territorial power had been successful in wresting power from decentralized social worlds. Local social customs imbedded in religious and folk beliefs prevailed. "Kinship and vassalage were knit by companionage".[8] The dominance of vassalage was personal and of a quasi-familial character. Tradition prevailed and neither land nor labor were market commodities. An ethic of shared responsibility permeated the base of kin solidarity and the methods of restoring peaceful relations. There persisted a collective consciousness such that the fear of bringing dishonor upon one's kindred regulated behavior.[9] The behavior of each implicated the honor of all. Disputes were settled by collective oath helping, voluntary compensation or collective battle.[10] Feuds, vendettas, kin vengeance and protection made indistinguishable the separation of "crime" and "punishment."

In the second feudal age feudal institutions began to disintegrate while the institutions of private property, entrepreneurial activity, the market, and the "rational" state grew. The real property holdings of the European monarchs fell to the merchants as collateral for funding each war. Land became private property. Serfs were expelled from the land. The feudal state cut its cord with kinship and affixed itself to the interests of capital. The medieval cities which Kropotkin described so appreciatively were crushed by this monarchical and entrepreneurial alliance. Their autonomy, mutual aid, and collective lifestyle were submerged in the thunderous sea of the mercantile state.

As the state began to obtain a monopoly in the market of reprisal, the ethic of shared responsibility began to erode. Violations of criminal law were defined as harms against the state.[11] Attempts by kin, and individual parties other than the state to settle disputes, forgive or engage in restitutions, or reprisals, challenged this monopoly and were made to violate criminal law. The state came to monopolize the power to create and impose criminal law, the substance of which was not only woven from the passing feudal fabric (blood harms) but from mercantile fabric as well (theft, robbery, burglary).

Violations of private property and generally the very directions in which the social order could develop were prescribed and controlled by penal sanction. "Criminal laws strangled the ability of the lower classes (those alienated from landed feudal ties who had migrated to cities as 'free labor') to possess tools or capital goods, raw materials, and also, under pain of heavy penal sanction, forbade association with guild masters."[12] Penal sanctions, in the controlling interest of merchants, guaranteed a labor force and created two classes of person – those bound only by the non-punitive civil law, that is, the merchant class, and those bound by criminal laws and penal sanctions, the disenfranchised labor class. The alliance of the state and capital constructed law to govern both *within*-class (civil) and *between*-class (criminal) relationships. The system of "justice" constructed exempted the ruling class from incrimination by the state and exempted the state from self-incrimination. At the same time, it instituted class justice, the subjection and incrimination of non-elites.[13] It forbade individuality at its most fundamental, by directing persons as to their degree of engagement in the material world. The symbolic contest and its mystification ceremonies was begun, as the labor class began to lose its power to create.

The legal mechanizations discussed are no longer explicitly class-exclusive nor are they as simple. The rigid duality of laws has cracked, engulfing the owners and entrepreneurs of capital within the web of criminal law. But this engulfing is largely symbolic. "As long as crimes among the corporate class tend to harm members of other classes, like those in the 'consuming' class, the state will not spontaneously move to prevent those crimes from taking place. On the other hand, as Paul Sweezy especially has argued, the state may be presumed to prosecute the wealthy if their criminal practices become so egregiously offensive that their victims may move to overthrow the system itself. In those cases, the state may punish individual members of the class in order to protect the interests of the entire class."[14] For the rich, the demand is for a noblesse oblige propriety on a kind of administrative level, self-management with respect to greed lest the symbolic world be exposed and begin to disintegrate from challenge.

THE ELITE, THE STATE

The state, in addition to an occasional symbolic criminalization from among ruling class members, attempts to forestall ruling class opposition through bureaucratic regulation, new law without penal sanction. Antitrust, antipollution, industrial and product safety legislation, and consumer protection laws, are examples wherein the gap between statute and enforcement is cavernous.[15] Selective enforcement shields claims of selective legislation which arouse greater public awareness of injustice.[16] If enforcement is inadequate the state can argue for more state enforcers, enlarging the state and its shielding capacity.

This self-generating pattern is congruent with the belief that inequities and injustices can be resolved or rectified by legislation, study commissions leading to new legislation, or newly created state bureaucracies. The invalidity of this pattern ironically places the belief/institution, the nation state or nationalism, in conflict with the belief/institution, capitalism or private property. The recent development of the transnational corporation jeopardizes the national interests of any one state. Therefore new institutional patterns and beliefs must arise from this conflict. These are quite clearly manifest in inequities of distribution of food and energy among the earth's people. The nation-state-capital conflict involves a questioning of national, private, or human "ownership" of natural resources (oil, climate). It involves a questioning of national, private, or human distributive control over life-sustaining energies. It questions and challenges "nationalism" and "private property" as beliefs/institutions. Will an immunity from state penal sanction continue to protect capitalists, in transnational or even national corporations? Will the state, through its militarism, continue to protect private extractions, exploitations, and markets in transnational or national colonies? Can those who through monopolization control economic and coercive power continue to immunize themselves from legal sanction?

At present, the state exempts itself from responsibility for its social harms. Because it is *the* definer of crime, *the* imposer of penal sanctions, and *the* politicality, its harms are beyond incrimination. It is not responsible for crimes committed by persons. Its reprisals, penal sanctions, are imposed upon those subject to incrimination *without* impunity. The behavior of its subjects, enemies, foreign and domestic, are definable as crime. The state, then, which invents crime, exempts itself. Its own acts are excusable, not subject to penal sanction.[17] Its own harms are defined as acceptable, as "non-harms."

As the form of the state varies, the substance of criminal law, crime, and penal sanction vary also. Capitalist, fascist, party dictatorship and welfare states expand, contract, create, and market their own particular brand of crime and penal sanction, those that fit production mythologies. No matter the form, the state seeks to monopolize consciousness and social life in the interests of the ruling few, to maintain hegemony, hierarchy and authority. The state thereby incriminates ideas, institutions, and social acts and actors which pose an institutional threat of disclosure or reprisal against the state. The ideas of individual or shared responsibility are manipulated to correspond to and help maintain their respective ideological state form (e.g. capitalist, fascist, party dictatorship, communist). The ideas of authority and hierarchy are carefully protected as basic to the idea of state. The differentiation between crime and "punishment" is manufactured and mystified to secrete the interests, power, and rule of the few.

The Non-Elite

On the other end of the complex legal duality, the criminal law has become increasingly important. The cumulative effect of the patterns of crime, violence, prosecution, punishment and state dependency (welfare) play a significant role in helping legitimize and stabilize new forms of capitalist or party dictatorship state arrangements. The aim of the processing of specific kinds of "problemed" persons, problemed in terms of personally defined pathology, is either to render them incapable of political, social or moral activity or to brainwash them into an active support of the status quo! This neutralization is provided by convincing many otherwise politically available persons that they have personal problems that have nothing to do with political process or social power.[18] Millions of persons are taught and processed to believe or fear they are psychiatrically "sick", that "something is wrong with *them*". They are rendered unconscious morally and socially and the seeds of revolution that exist in all of us are drowned in confusion about what is real and life-giving.

Law, with its carpetbag of incrimination processes, and ideologies of science concretized into programs, focus on the irresponsibilities of the individual, his or her inadequacies, or his or her mental, biological or cultural inferiority. The helping hand of the pathologists makes private problems of public social issues.[19] The pool of persons available for or conscious of hypermoral politics or social reconstruction is reduced.[20]

Evidence for the validity of this function of legal or scientific ideology can be found in the history of the welfare-warfare state's war on poverty.[21] Funded efforts to organize the local community in rent strikes, local control of schools, police and welfare-state programs were terminated budgetarily,[22] sabotaged programatically,[23] and discredited intellectually.[24] The social power and sense of community developed through these organizational efforts were political dynamite – threatening on a local and national level. We find only individualistic, "pick-ya'self-up-by-ya'-bootstraps" and "criminal potential" assessment programs surviving in the adjusted war on the exploited, oppressed poor.

This endpoint of the legal duality, the processing of persons as "deviant" or "criminal," is critically symbolic. This processing upholds the economic and political interests of the ruling few, creating and playing on the interests of one set of persons against another in continual civil war. The daily reported processes of criminal control present distortions, evidence for the creation and maintenance of racism, classism and conceptions of the poor as chislers, violent, lazy, or ignorant. These processes confirm the function for many of "blaming the victim", hiding the victimizer.[25] They serve to propagate a more or less permanent barnyard of creatures for slaughter. Lofland:

"Without a conception of deviant types of persons (and, therefore, without the existence of 'deviants'), how effectively might
the boundaries be drawn between the 'good life' and the 'bad
life'? How effectively might the limits of acceptable behavior be
dramatized and communicated without a continuing supply of
'degenerate' sorts who personify all that which is to be avoided?
Without a conception of deviant types of persons (and therefore
without the existence of 'deviants'), how effectively might a population discharge the inevitable residue of hostility and frustration
arising out of a warfare socialization and out of the struggles of
everyday life?
"Deviant persons provide convenient objects for the venting of
hostility in the classic scapegoat manner and, at the same time,
make possible the affirmation of the normality of the prosecutors,
the sanctity of the eternal Star Chamber. As Coser observes: 'It is
against the ground of their deviance that the righteous achieve
the comforting affirmation of their normality. Inasmuch as "our"
innocence is contingent upon "their" guilt, dereliction by others
provides occasion for self-congratulations.'[26] Without a conception of deviant types of persons (and, therefore, without the
existance of deviants), how effectively might a sense of solidarity
– of common moral community – be sustained? How effectively
might the otherwise conflicting cleavages of class, religion, sex,
age, race, occupation and the like be overridden? The very existence of deviant types provides a common enemy against which
otherwise conflicting groups can unite, a function served also by
the existence of chronic international conflict, especially war. If
defining persons as deviant serves such functions more effectively
than does railing against acts, then we need not be surprised by a
massive lack of interest in transforming 'deviant types' into nor-
mals."[27]

In the asking of these questions and the presentation of
these social reflections much more can be inferred; for example:
(1) Without the continual processing of persons as deviant
a population might direct the "inevitable discharge of hostility and frustration arising out of a warfare socialization

85

[that is, repression] and out of the struggles of everyday life" (that is, exploitation) *on to those in power*.

(2) The venting of hostility on other peoples (nation-state persons) might serve to take the steam out of domestic strife and might serve to criminalize domestic political and social opposition.

(3) The cleavages of class, age, sex, religion, and race are useful cleavages in diverting energies. (Note: Diversion by class cleavage refers to pitting the so-called "middle" class against the working class in the struggle for scarce resources, or jobs (affirmative action, quotas, racial preference in hiring and promotion or admission to law or medical school, etc.) It is a diversion from the reality that both the "middle" and the working class are similarly located with regard to the means and distribution of production.) These cleavages reflect or mirror legal processes in defining persons as deviant. Old persons are to be segregated, isolated from others, or left in the care of the "beneficent" state, as they are no longer "productive" or handsome. Women are to be defined as objects to be exploited sexually, economically and psychically. Conceptions of male and female reflect the forms of domination in the social order while concealing class rule. Women are conceived as inferior, passive, "unemployed." These cleavages certainly provide a fragile base for social solidarity!

(4) Only a truncated, distorted sense of community can arise from such cleavages. Correspondingly, only a very fragile personality structure, identity or self-concept can be built on the base of superiority/inferiority and competition. What degree of psychic strength emerges from a self-conception rooted in the illusive, transparent, and temporary state of comparison? What kinds of actions come from those for whom identity (self-"worth") rests on the backs of others, on others' failures and misery, which they knowingly create and perpetuate – actions which lead them through the processes of competition to defeat, and to themselves being processed as deviant?

If it is not "criminal" processing which hovers over such persons, it is being "economically" processed through replacement, forced retirement and unemployment until they are cast upon the top of the human scrap heap as one more useless element. If it is not economic processing, then it is forced invasion in the realm of social bonds, interference with relationships between self and others. The self becomes distorted and one's acts and relationships initiate responses calling for "mental health" processing. What quality of self can be maintained on the basis of competition and exploitation? What degree of trust, mutual aid, freedom and relational diversity is possible within such a self-construction?

(5) Is it true that the processes of criminal control provide the continual contrast without which the reward structure would have little meaning?[28] If so, who controls the reward structure? Is it forced and external to the experiences of community life? Or does it stem from the personal revelations of community members, based upon the freedom to be oneself, to work and act on one's own conceptions of the world, to become an "artist"?

Ideological Mechanisms
Criminalization processes are but one way of designating deviance. There are others, each different one having its own history and uniqueness dependent upon the power, organization and production designs of its operators.

Persons who have been designated as "problems" by those with power have received numerous labels over time. Those who posed a normative threat to localized religious ruling elites in the colonial United States were designated sinners, witches or heretics (religious designation), and met with whippings, brandings, banishment, and even death. Those who posed a normative threat in an earlier capitalist-state alliance (late 1800s to 1940) were designated criminal (legal designation) and imprisoned for economic exploitation in the production labor systems of lease, contract, piece-price, state-account and state-use. Those who pose a normative threat to party dictatorship or welfare-scientific states are designated patients or mentally ill persons (medical/science designation). Those who refuse to accept the conditions of the welfare-state megamachine are sifted, sorted and diagnosed until they reach the components of the paper by which they are processed. They are then resocialized, treated-cured, or hospitalized for therapy and repoliticalization (that is, active support for the party or "correct line"). They are acted upon until they are receptive to the modern state, which is tantamount to social lobotomization.

Criminalization processes yield legal designations and are historically tied to legal institutions, ideologies and instruments. Legal designations are not necessary, but they are sufficient designations for maintaining power. Legal hearings and processes are acceptable sufficient processes for determining the degree of normative threat persons pose. Religious, medical or psychiatric classification schemes and processes are their functional equivalents.

When being processed, the repentant deviant affirms the beliefs and embraces the institutions in question. The sick deviant no longer calls state beliefs into question. The enemy deviant poses a threat to the normative order of the ruling elite.[29] He challenges the legitimacy of their order, their authority, their beliefs and interests. Thus, when the legitimacy of specific elites or more especially their beliefs (private property, authority) are threatened, the elite act to discredit, sabotage, incapacitate, or murder enemy deviants and/or their collective movements.

It is more subtle and effective, however, for those in power to maintain social control by channeling deviance, directing it, and diverting it away from forms that might call into question their beliefs, their legitimacy, or that might usurp their power. Two sets of such mechanisms involved are, those that *insulate* challenges and render conflict latent, and those that *isolate* challenges by forestalling the development of challengers, of competing groups and ideologies.[30] Let us look at each in turn.

Insulating Mechanisms
Where conflict is rendered latent by insulating mechanisms of social control, these function as safety valves, releasing strains

and pressures from the institutional order. For example, religious rituals and other authority-controlled ceremonies serve to organize emotional tensions and check disruptive tendencies or to confine them temporally.

The economically created extension of "childhood" has led to the segregation of youth and the development of a youth subculture. The potential threat of a youth subculture has, however, been countered by extending formal education, developing military conscription and placing youth under the ideological control of adults who can contain, channel or supervise the forms that youthful rebellion, expression, and adjustment to becoming "adult" take. The extended maturation process, its institutionalization, and the "safety valve" concept of diminished responsibility, divert the activity of youth into frivolous action rather than into the development of serious personal consciousness and efforts towards social change.[31] Youth are directed, encouraged and exploited into non-threatening, energy draining activities such as drugs, sports, music, sex, and formal education. These activities, rather than being composites of culture, are bounded in total institutions wherein youth are swallowed, engulfed and detained.

In the economic sphere both "illegal" gambling and "legal" state-controlled gambling (lotteries) hold out hope, and release pressures from an exploitative economy.[32] Gambling is a safety valve for the American dream. It channels the responses and coping mechanisms of the economically exploited, and at the same time exploits them further, while the pushers of the American dream flourish in style. Allowing economically deprived persons to loot, or redistribute property from local merchants during riots truncates more serious challenges to absentee ownership, to non-local community control, to authority, to capitalism and to private property itself. State commissions (for example, the Kerner Commission) can *in retrospect* "study" the situation and issue words indicting individualistic racist attitudes and inequities of housing.

Isolating Mechanisms

Whereas insulating mechanisms serve to protect the ruling elite and their ideas from more serious challenge, isolating mechanisms attempt to prevent the formation of groups in which greater support for challenge can be developed. If "deviant" groups do form, isolating mechanisms are activated in an attempt to prevent them making a successful claim to legitimacy.[33]

A major mechanism for preventing the formation of support groups is the formulation of an ideology which isolates individuals from one another. Criminalizing individuals, and constructing or maintaining specific forms of ideology that place the cause for behavior in the individual are also common mechanisms. Criminalization processes constitute a form of extrusion from the group. The person is used as a "scapegoat," a symbolic representative, manipulated to better deter others and to strengthen ruling elite values. What happens to the person criminalized is secondary once the fool is set dancing before the court entourage. If criminalization is not an effective mechanism, then a nascent group is broken up by other means. Transporting gang youths to foreign turf, harassment, fomenting schisms within groups, and arresting "leaders" are but some of these mechanisms. If the group forms, then its claim of legitimacy must be quashed or circumscribed. This is accomplished through forming counter groups, through infiltration, through placing "agents" in leadership positions ("assuming leadership"), through countering ideological propaganda, and through "spokesmen" who engage in outrageous behavior, discrediting the movement. State activities employed in the attempt to discredit and destroy the anti-Vietnam War movement were typical of everyday state stratagems. Such tactics have been universally refined.

In directing or diverting "deviance" or ideological challenge, those in power prefer individual to collective responses because they are less threatening and more easily defused. Individual responses of a passive nature are less threatening than those taking an active form. "Deviance" directed toward persons is less threatening than that directed toward value patterns. Collective responses in which groups form and withdraw or retreat from the power scene are less threatening than those who engage power, the normative struggle. Let us illustrate. Religious groups, drug subcultures, or others who retreat into isolation, are less threatening than are community organizing groups such as the Black Panthers. The passive "schizophrenic" who isolates him or herself from others is much less threatening than the person who engages in individual "crime", and has the potential to develop a social network.[34] Violent acts directed toward persons in intimate relationships or even in the public sphere are less threatening than violence directed at the normative order, questioning its legitimacy. Words are much less threatening than deeds. When there are widespread problems, such as unemployment, victimization, disbelief in the legitimacy of the state or other institutions, or threats against the existing social order, the ruling elite attempt to centralize, to nationalize their war on crime, dissent and people. By centralizing crime control, "corporate capitalism (can) determine domestic policy in the same way that it determines foreign policy."[35]

By such insulating and isolating mechanisms, stabilization of the elite and of their economic interests is guaranteed against the interests of the non-elite.

PENAL SANCTION AND IDEOLOGY

The aim of all penal sanction has been the protection of the values and interests of the ruling elite. The various patterns of state, the substance of criminal law, and the forms of penal sanction reflect the modes believed best suited to secure obedience and control. The diversity of the forms of these institutions is rather like the variety of architectural designs from which Nazi concentration camp watch towers were constructed.[36] Yet, historically, specific modes of state penal sanction have been dependent on the ideologies and inventions of the elite, on those who have served them, and, as well, on the historically and geographically specific economic and social

91

conditions in which the elite have lived.[37]

We have already indicated that during the first feudal age, private arbitration, fines and penance were the responses to alleged harms and acts of dishonor. After the plagues of the fourteenth century when urban populations increased sharply, large numbers of persons, freed from serfdom, were refused work. They were outlawed from the guilds and imposed upon by the poor laws, having the city gates slammed in their faces. The breakdown of the feudal order and its effects on the organization and people of the medieval city threw large numbers of persons on to the roads. There they robbed, begged and banded together in vagabondage.[38] It was at this time that the private practice of retribution evolved into the substitute of corporal punishment, since most persons could no longer pay fines for their harms. Kings and princes sought to consolidate their power. In some cases many of the unemployed were recruited as soldiers. Greater and greater poverty accrued to the powerless, and harms ("crimes") of course increased. Gradually, punishments grew harsher and more brutal. Physical punishment, and then execution, which reduced the numbers of those defined as unfit, increased. Wages declined, fortunes increased and the value placed on the life of a member of the non-elite diminished acutely. Mass public executions thinned the army of vagabonds, paupers, and thieves. The royalty cleansed the streets of the unsightly.

As the land of the kings fell to the merchants, as "religious wars" depleted the European population, and as the developing economy of capital expanded, the worth of prisoners' labor increased. The supply of workers became scarce, maldistributed and restricted by law. The state slowly aligned itself with the interests of capital.[39] It responded by supplying capital, restricting the movement of labor, protecting monopolies, imposing wage scales, establishing a long work day, and prohibiting worker associations. What's more, it constructed workhouses for those who refused work, providing work for the emerging managerial class.

Increased trade in the Mediterranean provided a later use for prisoners, beggars and those who refused to work. The courts of Europe could not process persons fast enough for the economic slavery of the galley. Powering the national wars was useful to the state, a slow form of execution for those in servitude. The extension of European trade to colonies made transportation, indentured servitude, an increasingly useful form of penal sanction. "Between 1718 and 1720 transportation became the standard sentence for larceny and theft."[40] "Colonists" were shipped or deported, becoming a cheap labor supply for colonization and exploitation.[41] Transportation from western European states continued until African slavery, a more efficient program of indefinite servitude, replaced the domestic source of labour.

From Colonial Sanction to Fortress Prison

In the bustling frontier of the American colonies the pillory, stocks, ducking stools, whipping post, gallows, and cage all stood in the shadows awaiting religious sinners, wanderers, and heretics. Branding, ear clipping, facial maiming, tongue boring, followed by banishment, were common community practices as the elites drank tea in their waiting rooms, following old European customs. The pauper-stranger, the unsightly rogue evoked fear for the preservation of the community. The colonists did not expect or attempt to eliminate poverty or to reform the "criminal." They attempted to differentiate between neighbor and stranger. They assisted the neighbor and banished the stranger to an in-between-towns status. Locals were shamed, whipped, stocked; outsiders were quickly set beyond the community with a whipping or scar to ensure their non-return and to warn the people of the next town of their status.[42] Religious, supernatural determinism pervaded the prevailing conception of human nature; the saved should glory in the saved and cast out the social devils from their towns' souls.

This conception was consequently affected by the philosophy of the enlightenment, the idea that each human was a self-determining being, acting on the basis of reason and intelligence and therefore individually responsible for his actions.

Each chose his own fate. The free will of individuals could be influenced by fear of pain, which the newly emerged nation-state should evoke in order to maintain the social contract, the new social order. This new conception of human nature and the development of the idea of a social contract developed historically as an ideological framework for the protection of the rising middle class. Gouldner:

"The middle-class standard of utility developed in the course of its polemic against feudal norms and aristocratic claims of the 'old regimes', in which the rights of men were held to be derived from and limited by their estate, class, birth, or lineage: in short; by what they 'were' rather than by what they did. In contrast, the new middle-class held in highest esteem those talents, skills, and energies of individuals that contributed to their own individual accomplishments and achievements. The middle-class standard of utility implied that rewards should be proportioned to mens' work and contribution. The usefulness of men, it was now held, should control the station to which they might rise or the work and authority they might have, rather than that their station should govern and admit them to employment and privileges."[43]

Taylor, Walton and Young[44] summarize the social control, criminalization ideas that developed in this period as follows:

(1) All crimes should not be committed – a model which Matza designates as "correctional."[45]

(2) Pleasure and pain are the bases of motivation. Since all men are self-pleasure seeking, all are liable to commit crimes.

(3) In order to prevent a war of all against all, men freely enter into a contract with the state to preserve the peace. Human life, following Hobbes and Beccaria, is generally nasty, brutish, short, and encroaches on the lives of others.

(4) "Punishment must be utilized to deter the individual from violating the interests of others. It is the prerogative of the state, granted to it by the individuals making up the social contract, to act against these violations."[46] The state has the right to punish. "Every act of authority of one man over another, for which there is not an absolute necessity,

94

is tyrannical."[47]

(5) "Punishment must be proportional to the interests violated by the crime. It must not be in excess of this, neither must it be used for reformation; for this would encroach on the right of the individual and transgress the social contract".[48]

(6) "There should be as little law as possible, and its implementation should be closely delineated by due process."[49] "The laws only can determine the punishment of crimes. . . . Judges, in criminal cases, have no right to interpret the penal laws because they are not legislators. . . . There is nothing more dangerous than the common axiom: the spirit of laws is to be considered. To adopt it is to give way to the torrent of opinions. . . . Every man hath his own particular point of view and at different times sees the same objects in very different lights. The spirit of the laws will then be the result of the good, or bad, logic of the judge: and this will depend on his good or bad digestion; on the violence of his passions; on the rank and condition of the accused, or his connections with the judge. . . ."[50]

(7) Deterrence is the main aim of law and punishment. The law should therefore be public, understood and popularly supported. Not severity, but certainty, clarity, and proportionality will have deterrent effect. Therefore, imprisonment rather than corporal punishments should be greatly extended.[51]

(8) "The individual is responsible for his actions and is equal, no matter what his rank in the eyes of the law . . . (the act and not the intent is important). . . . Mitigating circumstances or excuses are therefore inadmissible."[52]

This ideology, while formulated and established to promote and protect the rising economic elites, recognized that man had to be protected from the state, the "excesses" of power and the arbitrariness of law and discretion. It also manufactured the idea that there is a consensus on the morality of and permanence of the then current distributions of property, power and life opportunities. It states that acts of crime are irrational, an unauthentic expression of experience. It also infers that the theorists, utilitarians, have developed expert knowledge (authority) with which to aid the state in its administration of social control.[53] Although this model has been historically altered and manifested in legal institutions, it remains a major means for controlling the non-elite, the dangerous classes, all of us.

Transported to the United States, this ideology was altered, moulded by the religious ideology of the past, the revolutionary war, and by the breakdown of Puritan order. The beginnings of a factory system were apparent. The religious community was undergoing urbanization. People became more mobile and the primary relationships found in the colonial village were evaporating.

In the late 1700s, the Pennsylvania Prison Society advocated and developed ideas which greatly influenced the methods of controlling "criminals". Prisoners were to be classified, housed, provided with work, and confined for indeterminate periods awaiting reformation. "Just" laws would minimize criminality. With confinement, useful work and reflection, new habits would develop. The forms of control would vary – solitary isolation, individual work, penance; silent congregate work, nocturnal isolation. The deviant was no longer a sinner, no longer a victim of unjust laws, he was now a victim of his environment and the fortress prison was born as the best bet of a messianic child of the Jacksonian era.[54] Rothman:

"Assuming that social stability could not be achieved without a very personal and keen respect for authority, they looked first to a firm family discipline to inculcate it. Reformers also anticipated that society would rid itself of corruptions. In a narrow sense this meant getting rid of such blatant centers of vice as taverns, theaters, and houses of prostitution. In a broader sense, it meant reviving a social order in which men knew their place. Here sentimentality took over, and critics in the Jacksonian period often assumed that their forefathers had lived together without social strain, in secure, placid, stable, and cohesive communities. In fact, the designers of the penitentiary set out to recreate these conditions. But the results, it is not surprising to discover, were start-lingly different from anything that the colonial period had known. A conscious effort to instill discipline through an institutional routine led to a set work pattern, a rationalization of movement, a precise organization of time, a general uniformity. Hence, for all the reformers' nostalgia, the reality of the penitentiary was much closer to the values of the nineteenth than the eighteenth century. . . . The prison would train the most notable victims of social disorder to discipline, teaching them to resist corruption. And success in this particular task should inspire a general refor-mation of manners and habits. The institution would become a laboratory for social improvement. By demonstrating how regu-larity and discipline transformed the most corrupt person, it would reawaken the public to these virtures. The penitentiary would promote a new respect for order and authority."[55]

In the first half of the nineteenth century prison reform and social control drew to it the keenest intellects and the most influential leaders of the "community." "No effort . . . financial, legislative, or philanthropic . . . was too great to apply toward a solution of the newly 'discovered' problem of the criminal and his reformation."[56] The forerunner of the fortress prison, the Walnut Street jail in Philadelphia, Pennsylvania, was based not so much on the "enlighten-ment" of Beccaria as on the need to control dissidents. The post-war (American Revolutionary War) period produced serious economic depression and social unrest among the poor. Many desired freedom and equality, to have the ideol-ogy of the war applied to themselves personally. Many devel-oped opposition to all political restraints. Some of the fundamental institutions on which the existing economic order was based were being undermined.[57] Rebellions were put down. Debtor farmers and "freemen" fled their creditors. With great irony the advocates of the fortress prison charac-terized deviance as the result of corruptions pervading the community. They believed that social control was breaking down. Offenders needed a setting which removed them from temptation; they needed regimen and discipline. "The peni-tentiary, free of all corruption and dedicated to the proper

97

training of the inmate, would inculcate the discipline that negligent parents, evil companions, taverns, houses of prostitution, theaters, and gambling halls had destroyed."[58] If crime was a symptom of breakdown in the community, how could the penitentiary reconstruct social structure? It couldn't! How could social and institutional breakdown be changed or reformed by reforming individuals? Very poor logic but very interesting ideology!

Punishment by private and solitary labor was actually devised to remove from public view "hard labor, publicly and disgracefully imposed" upon the poor. At this time, mass rebellions were occurring in Massachusetts, Rhode Island and North Carolina (1786). Moreover, prisoners (debtors) in Philadelphia, at hard labor repairing the city streets, drew large crowds who more and more frequently attacked the guards.[59] More important, however, was the worsening fiscal crisis of the Confederation, the scarcity of money, and the perception among the elite that thirteen sovereignties pulling against one another could bring ruin on all (Washington). The Philadelphia Society for Alleviating the Miseries of Public Prisons served to legitimize the ideas of a *state prison*, the separation of criminals and debtors and solitary confinement to hard labor. Significantly, the idea of the state prison reflected interests in securing an efficient government promoting conditions favorable to successful commerce and manufacturing, the unequal distribution of property. The new centralized powers of the state would guarantee the development of a new economic order. Through the issue of law and order, the confinement to hard labor, the "needed" apparatus of a centralized state could be promoted.

Dressed in humanitarian clothing, gradual legal changes (1789–94) finally directed that all persons in any Pennsylvania county convicted of any non-capital crime should be sent to the Walnut Street Jail in Philadelphia. A state prison came into existence when penal powers came to be monopolized by the state.[60] The poor, the dissident, the youth of urban poor were soon to be harnessed to the labor needs of manufacturers and shippers. Industriousness could be taught, profit could be made, control could be exercised.[61] The defense of "society" was for the good of the offender.[62] The advancement of commerce was for the promotion of the "general welfare."

Until 1890, the prison venture was a highly profitable venture for the state and for private enterprise, both directly and indirectly.[63] From the 1840s on, the United States was developing into an industrial power. Those who demanded separation, obedience and labor in the prison were concomitantly demanding the same celled regimentation in the factory. Inmate slave labor produced high profits for the state, for greedy wardens, or for entrepreneurs. In the lease system prisoners were "released" to an entrepreneur who exploited their labor, paying the state a fee. In the contract and piece-price system the factory exploitation moved inside the prison. With the rise of authoritarian labor unionization, racism, and widespread unemployment, the contract labor and convict lease systems were jeopardized and finally prohibited by statute.[64] Prisons never again showed a profit to the legislature, though numerous wardens continued contract and piece-price labor practices under the cover of legally allowed state-use labor.[65]

Could the fortress prison survive its own diminished economic utility? Was there an ideological thread that could be championed? Clearly. The fortress still served to incapacitate effective labor organizers and those who posed normative threats to the industrial merchant elite (e.g., the destruction of the anarchist labor movement in the 1880s, the intensive repression "culminating" in the Palmer Raids of 1919, the repression continuing still). Clearly, the modern theraputic, rehabilitative, positivistic model was readied for service to preserve the foundations of the industrial-legal order. In reality, the fortress prison had been a creation and elaboration not so much of Beccaria's image of human nature and legal codes but of legal mythology (a cloak of the consensual order) and the embodiment of capital interests in substantive law and administration.

From Fortress Prison To Therapeutic State

Mounting social-industrial strife in the late nineteenth century increased the numbers of persons criminalized and sent to prison. Large expenditures were necessary but unavailable for the construction of new fortresses in which to contain these persons. Prison populations, forced into idleness and overcrowded, posed the potential threat of riot and rebellion. To ease these pressures and at the same time retain the symbolic value of criminalizing members of the dangerous class, probation and parole were invented.

At this same time, science, the ideology of determinism, was taking hold. Its proponents held that each person was propelled by forces (economic, psychological, anthropological, physiological) of which he or she was unaware. Humankind was not capable of exercising free will; man was determined. The individual as a consequence was not responsible for his acts or character. Punishment, confinement as penal sanction, was inappropriate, deterrence foolhardy. Fixed sentences were counterproductive to the reduction of crime. The individual must be diagnosed scientifically and a cure prescribed for social defense. Indeterminate sentences were required to protect "society" and bring about a cure. Juries were unnecessary and inappropriate, as jurors did not have the expertise in human behavior to respond. The actor became the focus, not the act. The "criminal" was invented, for one's behavior, thoughts, mental health, attitudes, states were symptomatic of the person's essence, illness. The person accused of an offense was not a human person committing an irrational act, but rather, different, criminal (determined and different) or pathological. The "criminal" was not a person with an alternative or authentic morality/reality. He was undersocialized, in need of treatment. (Of course, science in the hands of *radicals* was a spur to the development of socialism. An exploration of social structure, social change, and human diversity-similarity upheld human need over duty as the basis of society.)

Could such an ideology help save the fortress? Certainly.

The most critical assumptions of scientific positivism are congruent with those of legal classicism, as we can see:

(1) Both classicism and positivism deny authenticity to an individual. The individual is either irrational or pathological. Both perspectives deny that fundamental conflicts of value or interest are possible. There is only one reality, that of the elite.

(2) The world, as it is, is unquestioned. The major values and institutions are assumed. In the case of positivism, the possibility of planning and distribution of knowledge is assumed to be equal, not hierarchically controlled and consumed by the elite.

(3) Both perspectives focus on the individual. One is concerned with symbolic processing for deterrence, the other scientific processing for crime reduction, treatment. Neither focuses on master institutions, power or the political economy. There is a separation of the study of crime from the theory of the state.

(4) Both uphold the sanctity of the expert, judicial (legal) or scientific. Both are based on authority and superiority.

(5) Both are correctional rather than appreciative models.[66] They are political in the assumption that persons should be corrected, and that the state has the right to sanction the individual.[67]

Positivism and its connection to social control was stimulated by the interests of the medical profession and the rise of Darwinism (1859 onward). The classicist position had already been dethroned, challenged by the early social positivists. The differentness and determinism embodied in the Lombrosian myth offered an escape from the implications and challenges generated from the assertion that existing social arrangements, social inequalities and hierarchial authority carry within themselves seeds which produce criminal outcomes.[68] Radzinowicz indicates that positivism had superior ideological efficacy, since a major political concern of the times was to hold down the dangerous classes. Positivism

101

served the interests and relieved the consciences of those in power. It allowed them to look upon the dangerous classes as an independent category – apart from current social conditions. There were two worlds. In one world, the dangerous classes, through their own moral shortcomings, were believed to have caused the wretched conditions in which they lived.[69] The elite could argue that the increasing crime rates and wretched conditions were not a result of capitalist exploitation or industrialization as Owen, Proudhon, St Simon, Fourier, Considerant, Marx and numerous others had argued. Those in power obviously did not wish to believe that their beliefs, that capitalism and hierarchy, were criminal in nature! They wished to conceal this and could find refuge in the shadows of another world apart from the unsightly.

One must also note that positivism's entry into "political control" followed periods of revolution, socialist and anarchist agitation and organization. The anarchists, especially, posed a threat. They posed a threat to the concept of *state* itself, and all organization of life based on authority. They suggested that new organizational life forms (structural reforms) were necessary in order to encourage the beneficial social "instincts" of man – mutual aid, spontaneity, honesty, love. Should it come as any surprise that those who write criminological history (state history) pretend that this period (like that of the feudal era) was insignificant, practically non-existent, in the history of humankind? What occurred in it, that the relationship between classicism and individual positivism (between Roman and British law) must not be learned?

The fortress prison would be salvaged quite handily by the new positivism. In the remoteness of the fortress, one could either pretend to "treat" the dangerous classes, or actually experiment on them as human guinea-pigs. For a considerable time the fortress prison was shrouded in the ideology of individual treatment, focusing on individuals' personal troubles, masking the public issues of social structure, racism, economic exploitation and other oppressive forms of dominance and authority.[70]

Psychiatrists, social workers, physicians, counselors, and

sundry other treatment persons entered the prison and juvenile fortresses. The child-savers were on their way. Delinquents and criminals had to be studied, psychiatrically, physically, chemically, chromosomically. Each one's unique, different characteristics must be located and rooted out. We must rid ourselves of the troublemakers, prevent the development of new "criminals" and rehabilitate the current deviants.

In the legal (state) sphere, belief in free will was adjusting to the era of science. Numerous varieties of mitigating circumstances were posed by lawyers as eroding, negating the responsibility of their clients. Pathology, mental incompetence, insanity, the weather, age, mental presence, even gender (female inferiority) was argued as affecting the knowledge and intent of the actor, making him or her partially responsible, thus diminishing penal sanction. The questions of right and wrong, "rational" person and "reasonable man," called for authorities, scientific expertise and superiors who knew what was right, who were rational and who reasonably would help the state excuse those who could pay for "experts," "defense," and control or treat those who posed real or symbolic threats, the non-elite. Bifurcated hearings, "humanitarianism," paternalism, diagnostic centers, token economies, group therapy: the list runs on and on. Science helped correct the "criminal," the "delinquent." The asylum for problem persons would make them obedient no matter its mode; school, mental asylum, prison, factory, government.

Social positivism developed as a companion thread. At this time, individual treatment programs were never fully practiced and rarely if ever showed results except at Buchenwald. Locating the pathology in the community rather than in the individual led to numerous attempts to correct and control "criminal organizations," leaving the macro-structure intact. Outreach, street-gang, detached worker programs which focused on the local community, deterred some specific persons from lives of crime but never dammed the flood of its production.

The underside of social positivism was organizing the local community, the belief that persons were normal yet forced to respond to abnormal conditions. When such organizers began to organize successfully, to construct local control and power, the programs were curtailed. Liberal reforms? Acceptable. Making prisons more humane? Certainly. Organizing people to construct a serious general social reform? No! Social positivists for years never addressed themselves to power, to national dimensions of control or to the state. It was not in their interests to do so.[71] They upheld the basic beliefs valued by the host culture and hoped that all could be assimilated into their pot. The radical critiques of Marx and Durkheim were censorially distorted, their concepts dehumanized.[72] We continue to live in a forced division of labor, in which our natural faculties are not being utilized.[73] In such a division of labor, forced rather than spontaneous, we are all deviants, subject to the "ization" processes (criminalization, institutionalization, colonialization, stigmatization) of the elite.

The social positivists posit that the "criminal" had had radically different socialization or was subject to a radically different set of forces, a radically different environment.[74] The deviant is thus viewed as a product of his or her environment rather than a rebel against it. The deviant becomes (we all become) a passive nonentity who is responsible neither for his or her suffering nor for its alleviation. The deviant is man-on-his-back, not man-fighting-back. He is certainly not alternately, dialectically, both. The deviant is (we are) someone who has to be managed, who should be managed better by the state's caretakers.[75] Consequently, attention is focused on the mopping-up institutions and their personnel who custodially brutalize us, self-interestedly process us, and benignly control us. Attention is diverted from the master institutions,[76] the concepts of state, authority and hierarchy. The social positivists present our actions as non-authentic. Our struggles for authenticity escape their analysis. They experiment, learn to control us better and protect the master concepts, the ruling elite. We are the passive man and woman; the manipulated man and woman, rather than the creative, acting man and woman. We are certainly not conceived of as alternatingly actively and passively authentic. Our actions are not to be appreciated, but, rather, corrected. Our diverse interests, talents, and emotions are not to be tolerated or encouraged, but simplified, homogenized and universally regulated. Our realities and attempts at community are not conceived of as dialectical, ironic or asymmetrical, but rather deterministic and symmetrical. How is it that social positivism directs us *toward* social structural change as an amelioration of our condition and at the same time directs us *away from* social structural change by conceiving of humans as determined?

"If man is merely an adaptive or reactive thing, a creature entirely of social or physical circumstance, how are we to explain the rise of new modes of social arrangements and new ways of defining the world? How do we explain the existing modes of arrangements themselves? Can we explain the new except as a necessary, natural evolution – produced by the old social arrangements themselves? Can explanations of this kind exhaust and even describe the range of human creativity and social change?"[77] Matza:

> "Capable of creating and assigning meaning, able to contemplate his surroundings and even his own condition, given to anticipation, planning and projecting man – the subject – stands in a different and more complex relation to circumstance. . . . Frequently man is wholly adaptable, as if he were just organic being, and sometimes, though very rarely, he is wholly reactive, as if a mere object. But mere reactivity or adaptation should not be confused with the distinctively human condition. They are better seen as an alienation or exhaustion of that condition. A subject actively addresses or encounters his circumstance; accordingly, his distinctive capacity is to reshape, strive toward creating, and actually transcend circumstance. Such a distinctly human project is not always feasible, but the capacity always exists."[78]

Law And Science Save The State

The themes of individual treatment (individual positivism) and individual treatment through the ideology of local environmental reform (social positivism) have led to two current stratagems. The first of these stratagems for correcting and controlling the "dangerous" is de-institutionalization. The second is electronic, chemical, surgical and mind/behavior modification.

De-institutionalized Control

De-institutionalization is often accompanied in ideology by decriminalization and diversion, the search for alternative management stratagems.[79] De-institutionalization means closing the gates of the fortress prison in favor of therapeutic "communities" in residential settings. It employs the strategy of halfway house and limited, controlled relations with the "normal" community, isolation from which proved so dehumanizing and "counterproductive." The new label is "community corrections." The reasoning implies that the community must get involved, that the members of the community are responsible, that the members of the community must participate in the control of its problem persons. The offender must be integrated into the local community.

This decentralization of institutionalization presents the appearance of local control (more mythology) but is a movement toward the welfare state. The program is institutionalization, its form (reform) is worse because it makes the problem (control) less stark. Small, residentially based "prisons" or institutions ("homes") which improve the living conditions of the captives take the appearance if not the heart out of the fortressed reality of elite control. *The community corrections movement performs for men what the community mental health movement performed for women but its management is less visually explicit.* (Note: The community mental health movement in the United States sought to deinstitutionalize the mentally ill – to close the fortress, dungeon, warehouse asylums. This movement was positivist and profession-service inspired. Its advocates sought to treat persons with "problems in living" in their "natural" (though distressing) environments; to provide zone centers or outpatient mental health services.)

People who live in the local communities from which

106

persons are criminalized have few resources and are organized neither to know these persons nor to control or correct
them. Many in these areas would not wish to participate in
this correction process, but of course many others would.
Many, perplexingly, see themselves from the vantage point of
"respectable society," of the "dominant culture," with the
eyes of the ruling elite.[80] People living in these geographic
areas might be described as collectively non-collective. They
are atomized by their interests, individualism, survival, competition and the macro-level institutions which are dominated
by the elite. The fact is that, among the persons to be de-
institutionalized, few could return to any "community." *There
is no local "community."* People in the ghetto, and increasingly
everywhere, have no community. They do not control the
substance of law, their schools, the police. They do not
control their economy! Community corrections, like community mental health, is run by outsiders, for outsiders, in
geographically decentralized areas (of the city). For the community it represents one more baggage of elite programs.
Those who are processed by the elite are processed not to
have community. One can't be integrated into community
when community does not exist! But this is the new language
of an ever centralizing welfare state. The social structure is
not changed: only the managerial mode.[81] Did Jerome Miller,
the Massachusetts Director of Youth Services, possibly hope
that community might be rejuvenated, stimulated or reborn
through his closing of the fortresses for youth in Massachusetts?

Behavior/Mind Control
The second strategy is behavior/mind control technology. "In
the very near future, a computer technology will make possible alternatives to imprisonment. The development of
systems for telemetering information from sensors implanted
in or on the body will soon make possible the observation and
control of human behavior without actual physical contact.
Through such telemetric devices, it will be possible to maintain twenty-four-hour-a-day surveillance over the subject and

107

to intervene electronically or physically to influence and control selected behaviour."[82] Cloaking their programs in legal assurances and proposing to hasten evolution along by altering man's biological structure, proponents of this stratagem ask: "What better place to start than with those individuals most in need of a change for the better?"[83]

Who controls, treats, conditions and demolishes whom? How and why? Can we rely on medical experts, the authority or expertise of correctional or mental hygiene specialists? Shall we call in judicial authorities, provide "community" review?[84] Are there any real differences in the perspectives held among these welfare-state authorities? Can moral and social issues be left to anyone or any set of them? Are there no limits to coercive treatment for offenders?[85] For us all? Can the offender be modified in the community? Can all be modified through mind/behavior control as we are now through information/economic pedagogics? Shall we all then be indeterminately sentenced[86] – our natural selves reduced to mechanics?

State Crisis and Resisting the State

To those who have explored, there have been no successful correctional programs. Yet, they have all been successful in retaining a pool of persons for processing. They have all drawn attention away from or aided the elite more directly by controlling those the elite wished to control and by upholding those values the elite wished upheld. The experiments, the stratagems of mind/behavior control lack ideological subtlety. Despite its continuing practice it has energized experts to dust off Beccaria. It is back to the legal model. At its best the return is a restatement of free will, the prisoners' right to refuse treatment, the sanctity of man. The dust cleared, the justice model[87] finds mind/behavior control aversive.

At its worst, the legal re-run advocates the incapacitation of the offender, putting him away for a "reasonable" period of time regardless of deterrent value. Increase the cost of crime to the offender, save the state.[88] Still worse are the legal marriages to the therapeutic state. This marriage concerns itself with protecting the "unfit individual against undue burdens and . . . guarding the state against the sapping of its reserves."[89] Even though treatment confinement might be longer and its effects more devastating and dehumanizing, compulsory therapy for those with "dangerous status" as operated by the experts of science/health is defined as and generally accepted as value-free or beneficient.

The juridical experts discovered with cunning effect that procedures to deal with "rational incompetents," dangerous persons, were civil in nature and thus they need not adhere to the rigor or charade of ordinary criminal due process. Insofar as the person was dangerous he or she should be subjected to whatever treatment is needed for social defense of the state.[90] In the therapeutic state one has the right to be different so long as one is benign toward the state and the elite it serves. The scalpel, electronic surgery or psychotropic chemicals await those who are designated "dangerous" in thought, belief, condition, or action. In the boldest irony possible, legal protections come to serve and support the therapeutic state and its exacerbated fiscal crisis.[91]

The fiscal crisis (expenditure increases surpassing revenue increases) is of course the product of the state's regulation-legitimization function in securing for the elite the appropriation of economic surplus. Capital-intensive growth is increasingly dependent on state growth. If national interests are to achieve supremacy over capital interests, states must either provide new investment opportunities for their state-based monopolist elites or nationalize capital. Inter-state war and the provision of militaristic markets are increasingly "unprofitable."[92] One possible domestic opportunity for capital investment is the direct investment of elite capital in the state itself. National defense and space exploration are examples. As the state expands, capital is being further invested in domestic political expenditures. Transportation, "education," housing, economic subsidization for the colonized poor, police, media, mental health, environmental protection, and other therapeutic-state programs are becoming surplus capital investment markets.[93] Prisons, state-regulatory bureaucracy, and behavior/mind control programs are additional markets. *The domestic political-industrial complex is replacing the military-industrial complex as nationalism and capitalism collide on a shrinking earth.*

Exploitation and oppression are wed in one institution. Capitalism becomes state capitalism, welfare socialism becomes the administrative state.

Yet the nation-state is itself cracking, breaking down. Multinational conglomerates, common markets, cartels, oil-producing "nations," the earth's economy is being centralized, monopolized by private capitalists and megastates. Horowitz:

"By posing on the national level the central issues of the international conflict, by linking the international struggle for self-determination with the internal quest for social equality and social control, the crisis of democracy increasingly presents itself as the revolutionary crisis of the epoch. The movement for the sovereignty of the people within the imperial nation coincides with the struggle for self-determination in the international sphere. Just as domestically the demand for democratic power is a demand to overthrow the corporate ruling class and to make the productive apparatus responsive to social needs, so internationally the precondition of democratic sovereignty and inter-state coexistence is the dissolution of the government of the international corporations and financial institutions which have expropriated the sovereignty of nations in order to appropriate the wealth of the world."[94]

Will an earth-state be invented? Is total centralization a necessary precondition for total revolution, successful revolution?[95] We believe not.

Can a legal-symbolic stratagem revived in the face of aversion to the therapeutic state prove as effective this time around? Will we assert our wills and create new social arrangements which contain no state, no mode of domination, no mode of prison? Prisons, old symbols of servitude, must not be replaced by new modes that promise only the "fairness" of punishment. Free people have no use for prisons, no matter their mode. Throughout the centuries, in all nation-states, the spirit of liberty, self-administration and equality has been crushed by execution, imprisonment and incapacitation.[96] The new modes of penal sanction and control in the new modes of state (party dictatorship, welfare, administrative) directly encroach upon the mind, encroach upon the continuing possibility of community. All forms of state, all forms of domination, all forms of authority, all forms of control must be resisted!

SOCIAL HARMS: A NON-STATE APPROACH

Is it not ironic that we have normatively arrived at an end to the state when we took the state as our initial reference point? Though we have taken the state and legal definition of crime and penal sanction as a reference point, we neither accept nor assume a state (legal) definition of crime and penal sanction. Crime and penal sanction are historically specific types of social harms. They receive their form and substance from the mode of state, the mode of law. The state and law are not benign inventions, as state propaganda might try to lead us to believe. Their mode reflects the realities of domination, power and privilege, authority, and sources of legitimacy manufactured by and for the elite. Taking the state, law, crime, and penal sanction as reference points forces us to demystify the social harms of the state. It forces us to explore penal sanction as a social harm unique to these institutions. If forces us to explore the other social harms which representatives of the state commit, such as genocide, assassination, taking others' lives in inter-state wars or on the streets within the state.[97] It forces us to inquire into the concepts of authority, hierarchy and property. It forces us to look at all social harms, since they are manifested forms of these concepts. It forces us to explore all those practices and ideas which negate equality, self-determination, liberty, artistry, the consciousness of life. We must of consequence explore all modes of dominance and exploitation (imperialism, racism, sexism, capitalism), their

111

bases and consequences.

Though the harms of state-defined crimes are a most serious aspect of human life today, even more serious harms are the genre of the state itself and those persons whom it immunizes from sanction. One cannot participate in the therapeutic state without realizing that persons with the greatest sense of sociality are resolutely criminalized[98] or submitted to therapy. They are too sensitive to cope with our exploitative condition. We mean those who refuse to persecute persons of a different color, sex, age, history, lifestyle. We mean those who refuse to participate in, or who protest against, the destruction of other persons. We refer to those whose talents are undeveloped, unappreciated, whose relationships with others are distorted; those who are exploited and passively adapt, mentally retreat; those who experience anguish in attempting to extricate themselves from responsibility for the inhumanity they perceive.

One must consider social harms in a context not restricted by legal institutions. One must consider the institutions, ideas and actors who deny food, shelter, clothing, health,[99] life, and economic opportunity as perpetuating, generating and committing social harms. These are the human life rights of all individuals. *We are intrinsically equal. We are intrinsically equal as entities, though each is unique in actions, expressions and emotions.* Our equality is based on our humanity, our freedom and uniqueness, not our strengths and weaknesses. The rights of every person are as unassailable as those of every other.[100] Any attempt to control another, to deny these rights to another, is a social harm. The fact of social harm is not altered whether control or denial is attempted by an ordinary "criminal," one's friend, a capitalist, therapist, father, bureaucrat, teacher, or agent of the state. Liberty cannot emerge through revolutionary violence any more than through statist penal sanction. Both attempts, being attempts to control others and deny liberty, are social harms, harms that are destined to yield further harms and modes of control.

Today as in the past much rhetoric is heard amid shouts of imperialism, racism, capitalism and sexism. These "isms" are

112

not mere rhetoric, just expressive categories. They are sets of attitudes that specify a mode of control as it is manifested in behavior, as this behavior yields social harm. A brief illustration will, we hope, indicate exactly how social harms are inextricably related to basic belief sets and values.

Sexism

Sexism has everything to do with concepts of male and female. It implies that either males or females conceive of each other as inferior-superior. It implies that young humans ("children") will be socialized and themselves create the reality of identity based on competition, the differentness and hierarchy of male and female. That sex identity is a salient critical category is learned, mentally and socially created. That sex identity is socially important is an historical and cultural variant. The belief that males and females are different biologically yet *equal* humanly is an historical and cultural variant. The belief that males and females are different biologically yet *unequal* humanly is, as well, an historical and cultural variant. The latter belief is generated by and generates sexism; the belief that males or females are superior; the construction of social arrangements which secure or perpetuate this belief; the acts which result in the control, invasion and social harms of persons of one sex on persons of the other. In our society at this time it is generally males who claim superiority, base their identities on maleness (traits/behavior they believe to reflect their conception of superiority) and attempt to negotiate social arrangements through which they can legitimate and act on their "superiority" to control, invade the liberty and humanness of females, to commit social harms against them.

Males attempt to support the tensions of their fragile superiority conception through the isolating and insulating processes we have discussed. They attempt to define, socialize and force females into: passivity and emotionality; into directing their acts against persons rather than concepts of male-female; into obedience through financial dependency and the "positive" differentness of femaleness, feminity, and into isolation preventing females through the division of labor, child-rearing and the nuclear family from collectively rebelling toward freedom and the development of a consciousness that reflects their humanity. The social harms of sexism are widely institutionalized in media conceptions of male-female, in differential opportunity for creative expression and in differential opportunity for varied life experiences. One's mode of response to these institutionalizations varies greatly with understanding, personal history, self-conception, consciousness and one's construction of personal relationships.[101]

And yet there are complex contradictions inherent in these institutionalizations and responses. One positive consequence is that females, being dependent on familial arrangements, are somewhat insulated from direct exploitation and alienation in the political-economy. The familial sphere remains one of the few remaining spheres wherein the pleasure and pain of mutual aid, solidarity, and interaction is experienced. The negative consequences of institutionalized sexism are seemingly great – anguish, loneliness, minimal psychic support, and exploitative invasions to which females are subject and to which they must respond. Sexism pervades all relationships in our society, and only most especially those relationships between males and females. When females are conceived of as objects to be exploited, as chattels to be used; when females are dealt with as sex objects and suppress their sexuality, social harms are evident. Inextricably woven from the dirty fiber of sexism is the crime, the social harm of rape. The belief in male superiority, the legitimized invasion of females, permits this social harm without much fear of disclosure or social sanction. Rape is not an inordinate extension from male invasion at home, prostitution, or an exploitative division of labor. It is a crime, a social harm of power, a channel for the expression of superiority perhaps undertaken by persons who are frustrated in their attempts to dominate and invade the dignity and freedoms of others in other life contexts. Are these persons unsuccessful in dominating others at home or in the economic sphere, spheres wherein they themselves are dominated? (It is possible that one of these spheres might be family relations, thus rape might be an act of revenge for maternal oppression.)

Rape is a widespread reality that flourishes in an institutional context of domination, authority, and superiority. Rape flourishes in the context of the belief in private property, wherein females are designated as property to be serially traded, swapped, used as status ornaments, to be dehumanized. Rape flourishes in the context of a polity (state) and an economy (exploitation of all persons as objects) wherein people are means to elite ends. This social harm is contained in and defined by our values, beliefs and the existing social arrangements of our social order. Gilmore and Selock:

> "The way to stop the state is to develop self sustaining forms of social organization based upon direct action, mutual aid, and voluntary association. The way for anarchists to help stop rape without police or judicial intervention is to educate everyone to the true nature and extent of rape, to organize concerned people in the community and on the job to make it more and more difficult for rapes to occur . . . to initiate some type of direct action (e.g. putting social pressure on the rapist by telling the community or fellow workers . . . and/or confronting the rapist and encouraging him to seek . . . help). Anarchists should join forces with men and women already engaged in this struggle, and thereby strengthen the numerous libertarian aspects already present in the anti-rape (and women's) movement(s). This in turn, will reinforce the anarchic prospects of a social revolution some day (soon), as well as finding the most anti-authoritarian solution that is presently available for ending . . . rape."[102]

We must recognize that rape is dependent upon sexism. All attempts at changing conceptions of sex identities that promote the authenticity of all persons regardless of sex phenotype should be encouraged. Altering the manner and typing in your immediate family and among friends, is important. Changing the nature of male-female presented in media, books and school is critical. Acting and living in modes which do not invade others' freedom of action and belief is more important.

115

"Woman Is The Nigger Of The World"

"Woman is the nigger of the World
Yes she is . . . Think about it
Woman is the nigger of the world
Think about it . . . do something about it
We make her paint her face and dance
If she won't be a slave, we say that she don't love us
If she's real, we say she's trying to be a man
While putting her down we pretend that she's above us
Woman is the nigger of the world . . . yes she is
If you don't believe me, take a look at the one you're with
Woman is the slave of slaves
Ah yeh . . . better scream about it
We make her bear and raise our children
And then we leave her flat for being a fat old mother hen
We tell her home is the only place she should be
Then we complain that she's too unworldly to be our friend
Woman is the nigger of the world . . . yes she is
If you don't believe me, take a look at the one you're with
Woman is the slave to the slaves
Yeh (think about it)
We insult her every day on TV and wonder why she has no guts or
confidence
When she's young we kill her will to be free
While telling her not to be so smart we put her down for being so
dumb
Woman is the nigger of the world
Yes she is . . . if you don't believe me, take a look at the one you're
with
Woman is the slave to the slaves
Yes she is . . . if you believe me, you better scream about it
Repeat:
We make her paint her face and dance
We make her paint her face and dance
We make her paint her face and dance"[103]

John Lennon and Yoko Ono

Freedom

The freedom of the oppressor, the invader, is critically im-

116

portant. In the pattern of sexism men are harmed as well. They are harmed because their sex identities diminish their self potential as well as that of females. They force themselves into activities and modes which are destructive. Exploiting others, directly diminishes self. Many men are not actualized in their activities. Some have the talents, the patience, and will to nurture young persons. Some have the talents for cooking, nursing and teaching from which many are self-excluded. In this sense we need human liberation from concepts, values and ideas which constrict our most joyous and productive energies. Men, as well as women, are constricted by sexism.

But acting and organizing to diminish sexism is not an end. Sexism is but a mode of, a reflection of, the ideas of dominance, hierarchy, authority, and competition. We must work, apply ourselves to diminishing all forms and arrangements which flow from these ideas. We must work toward altering the social arrangements of work and home life. We must change our ideas, discontinue being prisoners of our ideas, and act on new ideas.

Rape will occur with increasing frequency if our lives become more dominated, invaded by, the state, the elite and the ideas of private property appropriation, authority, competition, nationalism, imperialism, ageism, racism and sexism. We must devise personal codes of conduct based on non-injury toward others. We must strive to be a struggling, living example of human possibilities.[104] Through our attempt at good sense, affection, initiative, example, spontaneity, and co-operation, we must demonstrate the authenticity of life existent in non-hierarchical arrangements.

In our present social condition of massive exploitation and invasion it is not surprising that many persons choose to exploit rather than to be exploited; choose to minimize everyday life situations in which they are controlled, invaded, raped. In these responses we are at once both rational and emotional. Our responses are at once an expression of our circumstance and an expression against our circumstance. Acts and responses are undertaken; one cannot isolate emotionality from rationality.[105]

We are, it seems, capable of cooperation, sympathy, affection, initiative and spontaneity. We are, it seems, equally capable of coercion, selfishness, domination, passivity, unconcern for our fellow travelers in life. We need to organize our lives upon freedom, liberty, justice and equality, maximizing the first listed set of capabilities. Bakunin:

> "To be personally free means for every man living in a social milieu not to surrender his thought or will to any authority but his own reason and his own understanding of justice, in a word, not to recognize any other truth but the one which he himself has arrived at, and not to submit to any other law but the one accepted by his own conscience. Such is the indispensable condition for the observance of human dignity, the incontestable right of man, the sign of his humanity. . . .
>
> "To be free collectively means to live among free people and to be free by virtue of their freedom. As we have already pointed out, man cannot become a rational being, possessing a rational will (and consequently he could not achieve individual freedom) apart from society and without its aid. Thus, the freedom of everyone is the result of universal solidarity. But if we recognize this solidarity as the basis and condition of every individual freedom, it becomes evident that a man living among slaves, even in the capacity of their master, will necessarily become the slave of that state of slavery, and that only by emancipating himself from such slavery will he become free himself."[106]

We aim for and hope to approach the epoch of justice, mutual solidarity, universal freedom, the boundless expansion of individual freedom. In this there can be neither defenders of "order," nor guardians to speak for people.[107] We will speak and act for ourselves, for the freedom of each and all.

SUMMARY

Crime and penal sanction are both intended harms linked to the historical emergence of the formal, "rational," centralized state. As the feudal institutions disintegrated the monarchical and entrepreneurial alliance obtained a monopoly in the market of reprisal. With this, the ethic of shared or collective responsibility began to erode, the private harms of those controlled became harms against the state.

As the state (the elite) defines crime and imposes sanctions its harms are defined as non-harms, and its acts beyond incrimination. Also, the state (the elite) declares itself not responsible for the crimes that non-elites commit. Crime is thus conceived in personalistic terms, rendering us unavailable for political/moral activity – preserving elitist rule. In light of this, legal designations are not necessary, but merely sufficient personalistic designations. Religious, medical, or psychiatric designations are sufficient substitutes. Hierarchical power is further maintained by mechanisms which forestall the development of challenges, competing groups and ideologies, or which render conflict latent, insulating the challenged.

The history of deviance designations and state responses has reflected the modes believed best suited to secure obedience and control. The designations and responses have reflected the historically and geographically specific economic and social conditions of the time. Sinners, criminals, patients, and the poor/surplus persons have been responded to with banishment/brandings, prisons/factories, asylums/lobotomies, and welfare/consumptive worthlessness.

A non-state approach to the question of social harms has led us to analyze the institutionalization of sexism and the harm of rape. Rape flourishes in an institutional context of property, wherein females are designated as property, as objects – dehumanized. Rape flourishes wherein persons are in their sustenance relations, means, things to be used, exploited. Rape is a pattern of behavior which is the natural outcome of our root beliefs in hierarchy and property. To adequately respond to rape we must alter these basic ideas, our experiences, and feelings toward one another. It is not merely the victims or the harmed who are dehumanized by rape and sexism but all in its institutional clasp.

WHEN WILT THOU TEACH THE PEOPLE—?

WHEN wilt thou teach the people,
God of justice, to save themselves—?
They have been saved so often
and sold.

O God of justice, send no more saviours
of the people!

When a saviour has saved a people
they find he has sold them to his father.
They say: We are saved, but we are starving.
He says: The sooner will you eat imaginary cake in the
    mansions of my father.
They say: Can't we have a loaf of common bread?
He says: No, you must go to heaven, and eat the most
    marvellous cake.—

Or Napoleon says: Since I have saved you from the
    ci-devants,
you are my property, be prepared to die for me, and to
    work for me.—

Or later republicans say: You are saved,
therefore you are our savings, our capital
with which we shall do big business.—

Or Lenin says: You are saved, but you are saved
    wholesale.
You are no longer men, that is bourgeois;
you are items in the soviet state,
and each item will get its ration,
but it is the soviet state alone which counts
the items are of small importance,
the state having saved them all.—

And so it goes on, with the saving of the people.
God of justice, when wilt thou teach them to save
    themselves?

D. H. Lawrence

3   The State

Frequently, historical process in Western civilization is characterized as one of increasing rationalization. As the state has developed, rules of procedure have replaced the exercise of individual caprice, and nationwide governance has replaced the autonomy of small decentralized, tradition-oriented polities.[1] Modern administration has become rationalized in contrast to administration under feudalism or in the era of the absolute monarchies with its emphasis on tradition and particularism, and its identification of office with incumbent.

This "rationalization" of life has occurred through regularized and formally legal administrative procedures and through "professionalism."[2] Modern administration is supposed to be the antithesis of arbitrary rule. Its professionalization and principles of organization are supposed to do away with the intrusions of personal convictions and bias. Yet, at the same time, they design in an immunity or detachment from the desires, needs, or demands of the persons "served" and an assumption of consensual legitimacy for the hierarchy of authority to serve and control. Through the assumption of hierarchy and the ideology of science, the rationalization of Western civilization has sought the building of empires of machinery for destruction and for the dismantling of human personality and poetic consciousness.

Throughout the seventeenth century in Europe the idea of the state was quite intertwined with the ideas of family, property and society. The institutions of absolutism (Louis XIV) and the proclamation of national sovereignty (1789), however, "Postulated a conception of state as something separate and *sui generis*."[3] The state was thus conceived of as separate from family and separate from society. As an "independent" and separate, centralized "protector" of rights and enforcer of duties, the state became disengaged from the persons it supposedly served and from the multiple decentralized social worlds that statists wished to control and manage. The state has become a centralized social machine, constructed to induce and enforce compliance with the interests and dictates of authority. The problem for authorities or controllers is to themselves escape compliance such that they can creatively exercise initiative in meeting changed intra- and inter-state circumstances. Initiative must be taken continuously to innovate new stratagems that induce the compliance of the managed populations and other competing nation-state authorities.

The "rationalization" of modern civilization in this context has meant the centralization of authority and the rule of the few. At the same time it has meant the increased obedience and compliance of the many. The means for the securing of compliance and obedience has been rationalized, extended through the tentacles of the state's social machine. In this rationalization process, however, the ruling few have attempted to legitimate their power by claiming a higher justification for their right to rule. The governed have seldom been so docile as to not provoke such justifications.[4]

ALTERNATIVE STATE-ELITE MANAGERIAL IDEOLOGIES

All ideologies of management and control have in common the effort to make palatable the facts of authority/obedience. Thus, ideologies interpret the facts of authority/obedience so as to neutralize or eliminate the conflict between the few and the many in the interest of a more effective exercise of authority.[5] To do this, Bendix argues, the exercise of authority is either denied altogether on the ground that the few merely order what the many desire; or it is justified with the assertion

122

that the few have the natural qualities of superiority which enable them to realize the interests of the many.[6] These seemingly alternative managerial ideologies have emerged in the Union of Soviet Socialist Republics and in the United States.

The United States: Elite Superiority

In the United States industrialization occurred in the context of a weak state. In fact, the Confederation was abandoned and centralized because it provided a very inadequate and insecure environment for mercantile and industrial entrepreneurs. When rebellions occurred, militia could not be recruited to put them down. Merchants and industrialists had to resort to hiring mercenary armies to control the populations (1786), to assert their will and interests. The development of a strong centralized state occurred very gradually in the United States. Entrepreneurial elite were quite autonomous from state control except when the state served their need. The ideologies of individualism, private profit and the claim that the enterprise of the few would as well benefit the many obtained. The elite of industrial appropriators claimed natural superiority of character, intelligence and initiative. Their ideology promised the many that with proper exertion they would better themselves and advance to positions of authority. The robber barons and merchant princes were unhindered by the state in their appropriation of labor profit and extraction of natural resources. Where it was necessary to use the state and its legal machinery it was easily used. The exploitation of labor and the crushing of labor organizations through private police, public armies and the formally legal institutions of the state is painful and violent history.

Through industrialization, people in meeting their survival needs become alienated from their work, from their fellow workers and from themselves. The increased rationalization of the division of labor in industry subjected the worker to the degrading domination of the machine and the industrialist. Workers, in this process of labor appropriation and work rationalization, became isolated and organized resistance.

123

With the resistance, the elite sought to crush threatening groups (e.g. anarchists) and to restore the resisters to a more acceptable position within the unchanged industrial order. The worker was to be co-opted, reincorporated into the industrial social machine through a changed benefits scheme. Company and trade union consciousness (as differentiated from "one big union" or worker control consciousness) in its demand for higher wages and better working conditions in no way changed the conditions of capital entreprenurial activity. Labor was to be exploited, profits to accrue to the appropriator elite. Increased relative reward, "the decent wage," turning worker groups against one another, would diminish the resistance of workers. Managerial ideology remained intact. The Western ideological mode offers incentive to the mobile, individually rewarded worker, and appeals to legitimacy for a continued maintenance of the facts of industrial obedience. Economic (class) differences and those of social position are held to be open, and filled by the few worthy of position through exertion, natural talent and creative initiative. One is free to acquire and to achieve. The extent to which these myths are recognized as myths and shattered is the extent to which the state must grow to control the resistance. The school, the family and the media must be controlled to bolster the minimal truth encompassed in the ideology. New mandarins must search and discover natural inferiorities of black persons (e.g., I.Q.) or females (e.g. biological limits) to meet the ideological needs of those for whom they are employed. They must also find co-opting mechanisms through which the effects of economic exploitation, compliance/obedience, can be meliorated. The enlargement of the welfare state is of course such a stratagem.

The Union Of Soviet Socialist Republics: Elite Denial

As a critique of appropriation by capitalists and the managerial ideologies of the West, marxism (Lenin in particular) offered an alternative managerial stratagem. This ideology of management denies the exercise of authority on the ground that the few merely command and order what the many want. Citing the fact that in the pursuit of gain men had been alienated and subjected to the industrial and capital machine, Marx proposed the workers' state. Marx did not believe that it was possible to incorporate the worker's initiative, his pride, and cooperation in a common task of production as long as he was subject to the necessities of an organization whose operation and purpose were planned and conducted without his participation.[7] Thus, according to the practical plans of marxists (for example, Lenin), the commands of managers and obedience of workers should receive their justification from *common subordination* to a body which represents both management and workers.[8] Men should regulate production in accordance with a settled plan. All should own and plan as well as work so that all might become free. When men consciously direct their own actions and own their own tools, personal fulfillment will actualize. This particular managerial ideology took hold as an ideology of control and authority in the Union of Soviet Socialist Republics.

Industrialization in Russia took place in conditions vastly different from those existing in the United States. Industrialization in Russia was undertaken in the cultural and institutional circumstance in which government was the ultimate arbiter of conflict. The Tsars proclaimed this ultimate authority while recognizing, aiding and benefiting from the actions of the rising entrepreneurial elites. Exploitation and enslavement were widespread in industrial production and in the extraction of precious metals. From this alliance the Tsars prospered, maintaining their status as the "ultimate authority." From this exploitation peasants and workers alike demanded relief. But the Tsar was deaf and resistance mushroomed. The history of the revolution is one in which the ideology of self-management embodied in the free workers' communes and free councils of working people was defeated by authority-based managerial stratagems of the statist Bolsheviks.

Bolshevism in the Russian Revolution was the establishment of class domination. The *social revolution* (see the Kronstadt and Makhnovist movements) of peasants and workers, whose names were invoked millions of times during the entire Russian revolution, was used by the Bolsheviks as "the bridge to power for the new caste of rulers, the new masters, the fourth estate."[9] As has been well documented, statists fear free people. Their managerial stratagems claim that "without authority people will lose the anchor of sociability, will dissipate themselves, and will return to savagery. This is obviously rubbish. . . . As for the working people, it is precisely from the day when they become really and completely free that they begin to live and to develop intensely. The peasants of the Gulyai–Polye region made this plainly visible. For more than six months – from November 1918 to June 1919 – they lived without any external political authority. They not only maintained social bonds with each other, but they also created new and higher forms of social relations – free workers' communes and free councils of working people."[10] After the peasants had been defeated militarily, political control organizations of the Bolshevik party were instituted to control and manage the lives of persons already socially organized.

The second revolution, the political revolution, the Bolshevik revolution, reinstituted the state as the ultimate authority as was the past cultural pattern. The *social revolution* was captured by an external *political revolution* (counter-revolution) which was successful immediately in some regions of Russia but in others, such as in the Ukraine, not until 1921. With the success of the statists, the ideology was instituted that denied authority on the ground that the few merely order what the many desire. The resistance and rebellion of the many, the social life of the many, were reincorporated by force into a statist social order. The new elites, the new party dictatorship state managers, prevailed, with no little help from Western statists.

Since then, participation in collective ownership and planning has been a party, elite, activity. The promise of personal fulfillment has been unmet, as work is carried on in accordance with the externally imposed dictates of the single party. The historical events in "Russia have shown us the way in which socialism cannot be realised. . . . The idea of workers' councils for the control of the political and economic life of the country is, in itself, of extraordinary importance . . . but so long as the country is dominated by the dictatorship of a party, the workers' and peasants' councils naturally lose their significance."[11] "The dictatorship of the proletariat paved the way *not* for a socialist society but for the most primitive type of bureaucratic state capitalism and a reversion to political absolutism which was long ago abolished in most countries by bourgeois revolutions."[12] The administrative state interprets the facts of authority and obedience so as to neutralize and when possible eliminate the conflict between the ruling, managing few, and the ruled, managed, many. Like their counterparts in the United States, Soviet mandarins must continuously create new stratagems for the incorporation of the many, for the isolation of resistors and the insulation from resistance.

Today, "no one can deny that the centralization and magnification of power is greater, more immense, more all-pervading than at any other time in history."[13] In the industrial West and Japan, the economy has evolved from competitive, small-scale capitalism with robber/merchant barons into the large-scale, trustified, monopoly capitalism with gigantic industrial conglomerates and multinational corporations.[14] These facts, of centralization of power and of economic control, present a picture of swift drift toward a totally organized state that is eventually cemented by a secret police, a standing army, an industrial-scientific autocracy, and a propaganda-communications machine[15] pulsing the ideology of the elite. This concentration of power – military, political, and economic – of course approximates to that in the current party dictatorship states.

As the powers of the state grow, bureaucratic and administrative control widens as personal liberty diminishes. "Proudhon foresaw the greatest evil of the twentieth century: legalistic rule by civil servants leads toward state communism, the absorption of all local and individual life into the administrative machinery, and the destruction of all free

127

thought. Everyone wants to take refuge under the wing of power, to live in common. It is high time to halt: centralization has grown stronger and stronger . . . things have reached . . . the point where society and government can no longer exist. From the top of the hierarchy to the bottom there is nothing in the state which is not an abuse to be reformed, a form of parasitism to be suppressed, or an instrument of tyranny to be destroyed."[16]

THE NEW MANDARINS OF SCIENCE

In an age of science and technology it is inevitable that scientists, technologists and intellectuals will be employed as state ideologists. Physical, social and behavioral scientists are employed to serve in defense of and as creators of the policies of nation states that mask the special interests of the elite. In formulating policies, in receiving prestige and affluence, intellectuals, the new mandarins, are apt to "accept, not critically analyze or struggle to change, the existing distribution of power, domestic or international, and the political realities that flow from it."[17] Chomsky argues that intellectuals in service of the state adopt an elitist position, condemning popular movements and mass participation in decision making, and emphasize "rather the necessity for supervision by those who possess the knowledge and understanding that is required (so they claim) to manage society and control social change".[18] Bakunin argued similarly:

"According to the theory of Mr Marx, the people not only must not destroy [the state] but must strengthen it and place it at the complete disposal of their benefactors, guardians, and teachers – the leaders of the Communist party, namely Mr Marx and his friends, who will proceed to liberate [mankind] in their own way. They will concentrate the reins of government in a strong hand, because the ignorant people require an exceedingly firm guardianship; they will establish a single state bank, concentrating in its hands all commercial, industrial, agricultural and even scientific production, and then divide the masses into two armies, industrial and agricultural, under the direct command of the state

128

engineers, who will constitute a new privileged scientific political elite."[19]

Pannekoek, too, spells out the details of an ideology supporting the rule of the new mandarins. At this juncture the managerial ideologies of East and West meet. Pannekoek:

"It is not for the first time that a ruling class tries to explain, and so to perpetuate, its rule as the consequences of an inborn difference between two kinds of people, one destined by nature to ride, the other to be ridden. The landowning aristocracy of former centuries defended their privileged position by boasting their extraction from a nobler race of conquerors that had subdued the lower race of common people. Big capitalists explain their dominating place by the assertion that they have brains and other people have none. In the same way now especially the intellectuals, considering themselves the rightful rulers of tomorrow, claim their spiritual superiority. They form the rapidly increasing class of university-trained officials and free professions, specialized in mental work, in study of books and of science, and they consider themselves as the people most gifted with intellect. Hence they are destined to be leaders of the production, whereas the ungifted mass shall execute the manual work, for which no brains are needed. They are no defenders of capitalism; not capital but intellect should direct labor. The more so, since now society is such a complicated structure, based on abstract and difficult science, that only the highest intellectual acumen is capable of embracing, grasping and handling it. Should the working masses, from lack of insight, fail to acknowledge this need of superior intellectual lead, should they stupidly try to take the direction into their own hands, chaos, and ruin will be the inevitable consequence".[20]

The mandarins of the West, with their liberal ideology, aspire to a dominant role in managing the welfare state. The mandarins of the East, with their party-serving ideology, justify their positions on the ground that they are the few who have the expertise to develop, and produce what the many desire. On the ground of general welfare the many are managed, the mandarins rule or serve the ruling elite. Elites, those whom we might call political mandarins, in so far as

129

they are not scientific mandarins, use the terminology of the sciences to protect their actions from critical analysis – the non-specialist does not, after all, presume to tell the expert, the authority, how to perform open-heart surgery, how to build an atomic reactor, how to socialize children or how to starve a portion of the world's populations.[21] The non-elite, the many, should question neither the expertise of the mandarins/authorities nor their assumed benevolence!

Though there are differences in managerial ideology, the mandarins in the East and West find "justification for their special and prominent social status in their 'science', specifically, in the claim that social science can support a technology of social tinkering on a domestic or international scale."[22] The mandarin, then, claims "universal validity for what is in fact a class interest: he argues that the special conditions on which his claims to power and authority are based are, in fact, the general conditions through which alone modern society can be saved; that social tinkering within a welfare state [or administrative state] framework must replace the commitment to the 'total ideologies' of the past, ideologies which were concerned with a transformation of society. Having found his position of power, having achieved security and affluence, he has no further need for ideologies that look to radical change."[23]

Is it possible that these mandarins of East or West can manage post-industrial society, the paradox of scarcity in the midst of plenty, the many of the world, without social revolution? Are there limits to the capacity of the mandarins to use their violence and coercion without jeopardizing our survival, our chance for a decent existence?[24] Is there any ground for supposing that the power exercised by the new mandarins will be more benign than that exercised in the past by aristocrats and capitalists?[25] Will the new mandarins attack human freedom with a more efficient system of exploitation or manage a more humane and orderly society? According to Chomsky:

"Insofar as the technique of management and control exists, it

130

can be used to consolidate the authority of those who exercise it and to diminish spontaneous and free experimentation with new social forms, as it can limit the possibilities for reconstruction of society in the interests of those who are now, to a greater or lesser extent, dispossessed. Where the techniques fail, they will be supplemented by all of the methods of coercion that modern technology provides, to preserve order and stability".[26]

For the new mandarins, concern for human liberty and the ideals of a just society are to be treated with scorn, taken as naive, primitive, impracticable, or utopian. Technological, managerial ideologies and the authority-based economic hierarchies they protect dismiss all concern for liberty, justice, self-authority, and non-hierarchial forms of society. The new mandarins are increasingly unlikely to ask whether social life must be a Hobbesian war of all against all, if human nature must be confined to such a metaphysic. They are remiss from inquiring "into the contemporary meaning of Rousseau's protest that it is contrary to natural right that 'a handful of men be glutted with superfluities while the starving multitude lacks necessities'."[27] They are unlikely to "raise the moral issue faced, or avoided, by one who enjoys his wealth and privilege undisturbed by the knowledge that half of the children born in Nicaragua will not reach five years of age, or that only a few miles away there is unspeakable poverty, brutal suppression of human rights, and almost no hope for the future; . . ."[28] They are most unconcerned to raise the self-deprecating issues of how these conditions can be changed. They are most unfit to ask, "with Keynes, how long we must continue to 'exalt some of the most distasteful of human qualities into the position of the highest virtues,' setting up 'avarice and usury and precaution . . . [as] . . . our gods' and pretending to ourselves that 'fair is foul and foul is fair, for foul is useful and fair is not'."[29] The new mandarins are likely to and indeed *are* consciously creating institutions of socialization which should guarantee a reliable, uniform, homogeneous subject population. The human nature, "national character," produced is descriptive of the end-products of these socialization processes. In the United States self-interest, self-aggrandizement, and a withered moral consciousness are preferred. In the Soviet Union a similarly distorted moral engulfment in a false common-good ideology and subservience to the state and party elite describe the end-products of state mandarin socialization.

As socialization processes become maximally servers of the state, the elite and the mandarins, schools, media and the family will yield persons with vacuous moral percepts who "live in the third person pronoun, can comfortably press a button which disperses napalm over a village, then munch a candy bar . . . and feel no guilt."[30] The human nature desired by state mandarins denies to persons the reality that they are fallible and yet responsible actors. The state, the intellectuals, are to be repositories for the transfer of responsibility. Within such conditions the many are to identify with the state and feel powerful through its exercise of power. "Existence becomes to them inconceivable without the state to take responsibility to guide and protect. . . . The state protects us against nothing but responsibility. . . ."[31]

The state according to Schreimer is a human creation dominated by authorities bent on:

"(1) Maintaining by force unjust forms of property ownership, leading to poverty and the harm it causes (physical, mental, moral and social), pathological greed, fear, and the commercialization of all values; (2) Creating guilt, frustration, confusion, anxiety, and hostility with a multitude of arbitrary laws and regulations; (3) Helping to inculcate a false sense of values by emphasizing such irrelevant or harmful 'moral duties' as obedience to the demands of political, religious, or any other authority, however meaningless or immoral these demands may be; (4) Setting a demoralizing example of wanton brutality and indifference to suffering in its military activities, its economic policies, and of the nonconforming; and (5) Subverting community and personal responsibility by introducing its control into all areas of life."[32]

In this context the search of the mandarins in state think-tanks is not for truth or justice, but for *optimal operational alter-*

132

natives, the efficacy of alternate public policies, the management of the many and insulation from revolt. "The state is the most flagrant negation, the most cynical and complete negation of humanity."[33] As it provides the illusion of protection for some, it seeks to destroy, enslave, or manage others preventing the brotherhood and sisterhood of all from obtaining. The welfare and administrative states of the mandarins insure and "protect" against other statists at the cost of enslavement. The enslaved are institutionalized in regulated life forms which confirm dependency and encourage greater reliance on the mandarins. Kropotkin:

> "Today, the state has succeeded in meddling in every aspect of our lives. From the cradle to the tomb, it strangles us in its arms . . . it pursues us at each step, it appears at every street corner, it imposes on us, holds us, harasses us. . . . It regulates all our actions. It accumulates mountains of laws and ordinances in which the shrewdest lawyer is lost. Each day it creates new gears to awkwardly patch up the broken old watch, and it comes to create a machine so complex, so inferior, so obstructive, that it revolts even those who are charged with running it.
>
> "It creates an army of employees, spiders with hooked fingers, who know of the universe only through the dirty windows of their offices, or by their obscure, absurd, illegible old papers, an evil band who have only one religion, that of the buck; only one care, that of hooking up with any party whatever in order to be guaranteed maximum political appointments for a minimum of work. . . ."[34]

Within the order of the new mandarins justice is transformed into universalistic treatment, equality to uniformity. The mandarins pervert their "proficiency" in managing people and societies into a justification for doing so. The mandarins, more concerned with "progress," "experimentation" and knowledge, minimize the significance of the existence or fate of any single individual, any specific cultural or ethnic tradition.[35] Those who administratively or scientifically manage the lives of the many are now servants of the ruling elite, by the very nature of their work, if they are not in fact, the elite.

133

The Mandarins of Reform

A contradiction of state-capitalist or party dictatorship polities is that a system which violates human sensibilities engenders resistance among the managed.[36] In the past, when resistance occurred, the elite marshalled for their ends the intellectual mandarins of the times. Their role was to help create new management technology, new policies and apparatus, new social reforms. During the post-revolution era in the United States, the worsening fiscal crisis of the Confederation, the scarcity of money, and the perception among the elite that thirteen separate sovereignties pulling against one another could bring ruin on all, generated the Philadelphia Society for Alleviating the Miseries of Public Prisons. This elite lobbying group, dressing its policies in the cloth of social reform and humanitarianism, created the needed apparatus of the centralized state. This new organizational form would better provide an efficient polity, one that would promote and secure profitable commerce and manufacturing ventures while controlling and removing from sight debtors, dissenters from the new state, and the unequal distribution of property.[37]

During the Progressive era the corporate elite were again able to harness intellectuals and reformers to their ends, to bring together a vanguard for the building of the "good" community. The ends were stabilization, rationalization, expanded political economy and insulation from libertarian socialism, alternative, threatening, social organizational forms.[38] Within this era the National Civic Federation promoted certain social welfare reforms and by embodying labor "leadership" (Gompers) harnessed labor. The National Civic Federation sponsored the War Industries Board during World War I. The Federation and consequent government policy mobilized and regulated economic activity, recognized conservative, authoritarian trade unionism (in exchange for war support), and suppressed socialist and militant workers'

134

and people's organizations. (In particular, there took place the raids on and deportation of non-authoritarian dissidents. Focus on these "Palmer raids," however, isolates an event rather than analyzing the historical processes. The Palmer raids (1919–20) were not an aberration; not a single event. They were part of the still continuing processes of anti-alienism and antiradicalism in American society. War-time (W.W.I) Americanism or nativism, the concurrent changes in Russia (1917–18), a heightened concern for internal security (J. Edgar Hoover) and the protection of the political economy all intensified these processes and sold legitimacy for the raids, deportation measures, Wobbly incarceration, and immigration laws. These processes, of course, continue and have, we suppose, been most visible in the policies of internment (W.W.II) and more recently in measures taken against the Anti-VietNam War Movement.) Weinstein concludes that the success of the National Civic Federation firmly established the political and economic stratagem for handling crises of state and economy. The New Deal, Fair Deal, New Frontier, Great Society, Energy/Inflation Crisis, and Anti-Vietnam War Crisis were similarly strategized.

Domhoff's research into the post-World War II era supplants and verifies the stratagem of harnessing intellectuals and reformers to elite ends in domestic and international policy.[39] The National Planning Association, the Committee on Economic Development, the Council on Foreign Relations, the Foreign Policy Association, and the Brookings Institution were all financed by the elite. These groups trained government leaders, facilitated communication between corporate elite and academic experts and developed policies and stratagems beneficial to their interests. Economic elites, and those trained and socialized by such institutions as the Rockefeller Foundation, are destined to serve on presidential commissions, task forces, and special committees of the executive branch of the state. They control the ideological boundaries of such commissions, solicit only specific kinds of information, and generally pre-design the policy recommendations of such task forces. Cabinet positions and critical executive branch

135

advisory positions are now more than in the past the house of the elite. The new, specially trained, mandarins are positioned formally or informally in the key positions of domestic affairs (Moynihan) and foreign relations (Kissinger). Liberalism is crucially necessary to monopoly capitalism and the welfare state. The so-called liberal, reform, humanitarian foundations (e.g. Ford, Rockefeller, Carnegie) have been set up, financed and controlled by the largest corporate interests. In an era of great social ferment the ruling class needs a liberal movement which can act as a safety valve for mass discontent and thus deter people from moving toward effective social revolution.[40] As greater monopolistic entrenchment comes about, political parties take on liberal-reform rhetoric (Democratic Party). Thus, the modern state maintains its control over internal challenges by developing and institutionalizing the mandarins' wares, the new authoritarianism.[41] The latest preservative of the ruling elite's political and economic order is: a society managed and ruled "by a faceless and widely dispersed complex of warfare-welfare-industrial-communications-police bureaucracies caught up in developing a new style empire based on a technocratic ideology, a culture of alienation, multiple scapegoats, and competing control networks."[42] Gross suggests that future mandarins will probably produce:

"(1) increasingly differentiated armaments (including more outer space and under-sea instruments of destruction) that in the name of defense and security would contribute to world insecurity; (2) increasingly specialized medical, education, housing and welfare programs that would have a declining relation to health, learning, community, or social justice; (3) industrial products to serve warfare–welfare purposes and provide consumer incentives for acceptance of the system; (4) communication services that would serve as instruments for the manipulation, surveillance, and suppression – or prettifying – of information on domestic and foreign terrorism; and (5) police activities designed to cope with the new 'crime' of opposing the system, probably enlisting organized crime in the effort."[43]

136

THE HUMAN CONDITION – MISERIES

Is it not well recognized that the regulatory agencies supposedly set up to supervise monopolists in fact operate in the interests of monopolists? Farm subsidy programs benefit agribusiness while dispossessing family farmers. Urban renewal either reduces affordable housing and/or segregates low-income groups, densifying them into other fortresses (prisons)

Welfare-insurance survival programs regulate potential dissent into passive, personalistic, non-collective forms. The board newly created to oversee foreign and domestic intelligence operations is designed to remove from sight such operations. Is it not well recognized that social reform serves to strengthen and centralize power and control, to make a growth industry of authority? Is it not well recognized as absurd that the new mandarins should owlishly assure us that prevalent economic practices are not what they seem, but are in the long run ultra-humanitarian, designed to diminish the extent of human miseries?

The Source Of Human Miseries

But human miseries are not solely external to humankind, our character and ideas, and intrinsic to social and cultural, external controls. The human condition, the miseries, so defined, exist only within a definite moral universe. We define poverty as a problem, a misery, when it impinges on our survival, when it exists in the midst of plenty, or when it exists in a world in which universal plenty is a technological possibility (post-scarcity).[44]

Conditions of human life which we consider as human misery emanate from our beliefs, our ideas, our mores. Our ideas cause and define human misery. In the United States these ideas are private property, individualism, and, increasingly, nationalism and external hierarchical authority. Accompanying these mores are humanitarian ones, those which urge one to make the world better, to remedy the miseries.[45] What is defined as human misery stems from and is marked by moral conflict in the individual and social conflict among groups. When one defines poverty as misery one recognizes that the same mores (private property, individual self-interest) from which the miseries originate in fact continue to operate to limit any action which one takes in order to remedy them. The remedy for poverty in the midst of plenty is income redistribution.[46] But in the United States this solution is rejected at once because it conflicts with the institution of private property, and would completely disjoint the foundations of the economic order.

Yet humanitarian ideas and emotions require some response to misery/poverty. To paraphrase Waller, if the poor are willing to work, if the old live in strict monogamy and the young do not contract marriage until they are off welfare, if they obey the law, if they do not conceal any assets, if they spend absolutely nothing for luxuries (are not welfare cheaters), if they are grateful and not demanding, and if the level of welfare does not approach the income of the employed, few object to humanitarian aid, welfare, even permanent welfare, for others. The problem of human misery is thus confined within the limits set by the organizational mores.[47] Human misery is not altered significantly but rather further entrenched. The humanitarian wishes to improve the condition of the poor, but not to interfere with private property. The human misery which she or he deplores is a necessary part of the social order which seems to her or him good. Human miseries are not solved because people do not want to solve them. Waller:

"From a thousand scattered sources the evidence converges upon this apparently unavoidable conclusion, from the history of reform movements, from the biographies and autobiographies of reformers, from politics, from the records of peace conferences, from the field of social work, from private discussions, and even from the debates of so-called radical groups. Even those who are most concerned about social problems are not quite at one with themselves in their desire to solve them. Solving social problems would necessitate a change in the organizational mores from which they arise. The humanitarian, for all his allegiance to the

138

humanitarian mores, is yet a member of our society and as such is under the sway of its organizational mores. He wishes to improve the condition of the poor, but not to interfere with private property. Until the humanitarian is willing to give up his allegiance to the organizational mores, and in some cases to run squarely against them, he must continue to treat symptoms without removing their causes."[48]

It is not merely the elite who have an interest in the continuance of the organizational mores from which they benefit most, but seemingly many persons in the social order as well. Newly developed organizational modes for handling poverty are not a critical change, rarely are they consciously proposed as countering organizational mores. A real remedy to a perceived misery is likely to involve deep changes in our society, in our ideas and morality. Such change is, as well, likely to produce new human miseries, new wishes for the improvement of human life. So within the current order "no one loses by giving verbal expression to humanitarianism . . . but many would lose by putting humanitarianism into practice, and someone would certainly lose by any conceivable reform. From the powerful someone who is certain to lose comes opposition to [real] reform."[49] (By reform is meant a change in fundamental belief systems, mores – e.g. private property, individualism, monogamism, christianity and nationalism – both forms of external authority.)

The Alleviation Of Human Miseries

Though human miseries are defined social, historical and cultural variants, there are common sufferings which few orders have valued. "If human beings find it difficult to agree upon the meaning and causes of happiness . . . they find it much easier to know when they are miserable."[50] These miseries, energized and emanating from the ideas, beliefs and how the social order is organized, are war, cruelty, poverty, hunger, disease, injustice, oppression, and persecution for dissident beliefs.

Twentieth-century reality and historical recounting make

139

one question the human capacity for creating misery, our incapacity to alleviate it. Out of the efforts to sustain and/or subvert one's existing human misery (condition) social harms arise (cruelty and war). Moore's assessment that revolutionism usually generates only more misery, and that "successful revolution" usually generates more oppressive totalitarian-induced miseries is counterbalanced by the realization that to eschew revolutionism is to condemn ourselves to our current miseries – those sustaining the present order, the miseries (social harms-aggressions) induced by the current elite.[51] However, such an assessment and conceptualization of "revolution" is deficient in not stressing the fact that there have been no sustained large-scale revolutions against authority-hierarchy, the state. Revolutions which merely exchange political forms of control, management and hierarchical authority are hardly *social revolutions*. They are *political revolutions*, counter-revolutions.

It is quite clear from accounts of the social revolutions in Russia and Spain that the miseries of injustice, oppression, cruelty and aggression can be greatly reduced.[52] Only in social revolution are there real reforms, changes at the roots of organizational mores. Social revolution is a threat to all political authorities, all elites. These have uniformly responded and proved counter-social-revolutionary whenever and wherever social revolution has occurred.

To address the non-separable problems of poverty, hunger, and disease requires coming to grips simultaneously with scarcity and injustice. There is no question that a human social order concerned with eliminating scarcity would drastically need to restrict consumerism, and relate more closely to the scarcities of the natural environment (oxygen, water, unpolluted sea and earth). This does not however require the suppression or retardation of either knowledge or technology. Bookchin, arguing as socialists have for many years, presents a succinct documentation that we now, technologically, exist in a post-scarcity condition.[53] However, the potentialities of post-scarcity are neither socially realized nor are they allowed politically. It is not the alleviation of scarcity and injustice

140

which raises the spectre of massive centralized control[54] but rather the ideology and interests of elites, political and economic. Both the privatization of technology, natural and human resources, food supplies, and their political control require centralized coordination and control. The elimination of scarcity itself does *not* require such coordination or control.

There is no question that economic elites and their political mates operate to perpetuate the prevailing distributions of inequities and miseries. They together formulate policies consciously designed to starve whole populations of the world. The extension of survival to these persons, or rather the prevention of their survival, is a dis-economy of scale to multinational corporate capital elites. The party dictatorship state, as well, proves itself unacceptable for eliminating misery, not because it is incapable of nationally reducing scarcity but because it requires a repressive apparatus to do so. The party dictatorship state thus reduces scarcity but increases injustice and oppression through its apparatus of managing, socializing and monopolizing force.

SPIRITUAL REVOLUTION: ORGANIZING SOCIETY

We must, as a consequence, search for other life-organization forms within which scarcity can be reduced without increasing other miseries in the process. We must understand that private property and the state are ideas that must be rejected and replaced such that social life is transformed at the root. We cannot, of course, escape ourselves or our experiences. We must recognize that our lives must, perhaps painfully, undergo radical change embodied in acts and new forms of community. We must recognize that the "means and ends" of our revolution must be social, that change must come first from within. We must recognize that many of those who cry most loudly that we must smash and destroy, perpetrate social harms with the intent (if not themselves harmed) that they will be the new mandarins of repression and management.[55]

141

We must recognize, as did Landauer, that we must organize not in the state but outside, without the state – alongside the state. We must realize that the actualization of ideas, organization and emotions of anarchism are present and always have been present, existent alongside the state.[56] It must be made conscious to everyone that we are the state and shall continue to be the state until we have created the institutions and relationships that constitute a just society. Landauer:

"The state is a condition, a certain relationship between human beings, a mode of human behaviour; we destroy it by contracting other relationships, by behaving differently. Men stand to one another today in a 'statual' relationship, that is, in one which makes the coercive order of the state necessary and is represented by it and in it. Hence this order can only be overcome to the extent that this relationship between men is replaced by another. This other relationship is 'People'. It is a connection between people which is actually there; only it has not yet become bond and building, it is not yet a higher organism. To the extent that people, on the basis of the processes of production and circulation, find themselves coming together again as people and growing together as an organism with countless organs and members, socialism, which now lives only in the minds and desires of single, atomized people, will become a reality – not in the state but outside, without the state, and that means alongside the state. This finding themselves together of people does not mean the founding of something new but the actualization and reconstitution of something that has always been present – of community, which in fact exists alongside the state, albeit buried and laid waste. One day it will be realized that socialism is not the invention of anything new but the discovery of something actually present, of something that has grown. This being so, the realization of socialism is always possible if a sufficient number of people want it. The realization depends not on the technological state of things, although socialism when realized will of course look differently, begin differently and develop differently according to the state of technics; it depends on people and their spirit. Socialism is possible and impossible at all times; it is possible when the right people are there to will it and do it; it is impossible when

142

people either don't will it or only supposedly will it, but are not capable of doing it."[57]

The true revolution is one of spiritual rejuvenation, sharing experiences and experiencing sharing. Only autonomy, voluntary cooperation and liberty are acceptable human conditions within which we can eliminate the miseries and share the "happinesses" of our own design. Bakunin, writing on the Paris commune, expressed this as follows:

"I am a frantic lover of liberty, considering it as the unique condition under which intelligence, dignity, and human happiness can develop and grow; not the purely formal liberty conceded, measured out, and regulated by the State, an eternal lie which in reality represents nothing more than the privilege of some founded on the slavery of the rest; not the individualistic, egoistic, shabby, and fictitious liberty extolled by the school of J.J. Rousseau and the other schools of bourgeois liberalism, which considers the would be rights of men, represented by the state which limits the rights of each – an idea that leads inevitably to the reduction of the rights to zero. No, I mean the kind of liberty that is worthy of the name, liberty that consists in the full development of all the material, intellectual, and moral powers that are latent in each person; liberty that recognizes no restrictions other than those determined by the laws of our own individual nature; which cannot properly be regarded as restrictions since these laws are not imposed by any outside legislator beside or above us, but are immanent and inherent, forming the very basis of our material, intellectual and moral being – they do not limit us but are the real immediate conditions of our freedom."[58]

According to Chomsky:

"These ideas grow out of the Enlightenment; their roots are in Rousseau's *Discourse on Inequality*, Humbolt's *Limits of State Action*, Kant's insistence, in his defense of the French Revolution, that freedom is the precondition for acquiring the maturity for freedom, not a gift to be granted when such maturity is achieved. With the development of industrial capitalism, a new and unanticipated system of injustice, it is libertarian socialism that has preserved and extended the radical humanist message of the enlightenment and those classical liberal ideas that were perver-

143

ted into an ideology to sustain the emerging social order.

"In fact, on the very same assumption that led classical liberalism to oppose the intervention of the state in social life, capitalist social relations are also intolerable. Humboldt, for example, in work which anticipated and perhaps inspired Mill, objects to state action because the state tends to 'make man an instrument to serve its arbitrary ends, overlooking his individual purposes.' He insists that 'whatever does not spring from a man's free choice . . . does not enter into his very being, but remains alien to his true nature; he does not perform it with truly human energies, but merely with mechanical exactness.' Under the condition of freedom, 'all peasants and craftsmen might be elevated to artists; that is, men who love their own labor for its own sake, improve it by their own plastic genius and inventive skill, and thereby cultivate their intellect, ennoble their character, and exalt and refine their pleasures.' When a man merely reacts to external demands and authority, 'we may admire what he does, but we despise what he is.' "[59]

It is true that in the social contract libertarian tradition one addresses the notions of equality and justice, the problems of individual autonomy and social order. Yet persons writing in this tradition accept the notion that there are conditions under which inequalities may "*properly*" exist! While at last recognizing distribution issues as central, current social contract writers still serve to locate and justify those conditions in a society in which one can say that a given set of inequalities is just. Rawls's formulation aptly demonstrates this tradition:[60]

"An unequal distribution of resources or a given system of hierarchial authority may lead to greater productivity in a social system than an equal distribution or the absence of authority. If, and only if, that greater productivity brings to those on the lowest level more than they would have had under an equal distribution of resources or a wholly egalitarian authority system, the inequality is justified."[61]

Rawls's formulation assumes hierarchy and justifies it in terms of distributive ends. The state is justified for its redistributive ends, its utility in securing "justice." Through the

144

social contract, Rawls, in tradition, argues that individuals vest their liberty and sovereignty to the centralized state, which then controls inequalities, distributes justice, and doles restricted political rights to individuals. Liberty, freedom and self-autonomy are lost to the collective totality, the state, allocator of equity, primary goods (liberty, opportunity, income, wealth, base of self-respect), identity, and life itself. Can we, consequently, not recognize that liberty and opportunity for the individual are in inverse ratio to the power of the state? Are the miseries to be reduced or eliminated through institutional modes themselves inherently productive of misery?

Is each and every form of State not in essence as Bakunin described?:

"The State is the organized authority, domination, and power of the possessing classes over the masses . . . the most flagrant, the most cynical, and the most complete negation of humanity. It shatters the universal solidarity of all men on the earth, and brings some of them into association only for the purpose of destroying, conquering and enslaving all the rest. . . . This flagrant negation of humanity which constitutes the very essence of the state is, from the standpoint of the state, its supreme duty and its greatest virtue. . . . Thus, to offend, to oppress, to despoil, to plunder, to assassinate or enslave one's fellowman is ordinarily regarded as a crime. In public life, on the other hand, from the standpoint of patriotism, when these things are done for the greater glory of the state, for the preservation or the extension of its power, it is all transformed into duty and virtue. . . . This explains why the entire history of ancient and modern states is merely a series of revolting crimes; why kings and ministers, past and present, of all times and all countries – statesmen, diplomats, bureaucrats, and warriors – if judged from the standpoint of simple morality and human justice, have a hundred, a thousand times over earned their sentence to hard labor or to the gallows. There is no horror, no cruelty, sacrilege, or perjury, no imposture, no infamous transaction, no cynical robbery, no bold plunder or shabby betrayal that has not been or is not daily being perpetrated by the representatives of the states, under no other pretext than those elastic words, so convenient and yet so terrible: 'for reasons of state.'"[62]

145

The social contract, the state, is the spectre of massive centralized control. The resolution of injustice and distributive equity of post-scarcity primary goods is incompatible with such means, not only because of its spectre of control, but also because of its spectre of lost human quality – humane relationships, mutual aid, brotherly and sisterly warmth, and senses of responsibility and posterity. Our hope for the resolution of miseries resides in no actions carried out "for reasons of state." Our ideals are not fundamentally how we distribute wealth or allocate resources, for wealth could be equitably distributed in prison, and extrinsic resources could be allocated equitably through the apparatus of the state. Though Rawls lists liberty, opportunity and self-respect as primary goods, these "goods" cannot become reality either through the state or through its mythical social contract. Our ideals concern the liberation of the creative impulse and the opportunity of self-organization and the reconstruction of society to this end.[63] Our hope for the resolution of the miseries resides in people, us, in spiritual-social transformation, not political. Alongside the state we must build new relationships, social institutions infused with a rejuvenation of the spirit, the positive ideas of anarchism.

ANARCHISM

An anarchist social order, organized without hierarchical authority, "is always in existence, like a seed beneath the snow, buried under the weight of the state . . ."[64] It is a moral order in accordance with which people, from their inner convictions, act towards others as they desire that others should act toward them. It is a social order in which each is able to live and act according to his or her own judgment. It is a social order, incompatible with power, in which power is abolished through the consciousness of the truth that power is useless and harmful, and that one should neither obey it nor participate in it.[65] Power can only be abolished by our own minds, by our own consciousness. But what is this consciousness? Is it consciousness founded on Rawls's or Rousseau's

146

contract, Mill's ascendancy rights, Marx's socialism? Is it to be founded on the concepts of general welfare, justice, progress or the synergy of personal interest? Clearly not, for these foundations of consciousness conflict. The meanings of the concepts justice, general welfare and progress are understood in infinite variations. Tolstoy:

> "Therefore it is impossible to suppose that people who are not agreed amongst themselves, and who differently understand the bases on which they oppose power (if they do), could abolish power, so firmly fixed and so ably defended. Moreover, the supposition that considerations about general welfare, justice, or the law of progress can suffice to secure that men, freed from coercion, but having no motive for sacrificing their personal welfare to the general welfare, should combine in just conditions without violating their mutual liberty, is yet more unfounded."[66]

The affirmation that by each following his own personal interest (interest materially defined), just relations would be introduced among all, is in complete contradiction to what in reality has taken and would take place. Thus, according to Tolstoy, while correctly recognizing the spiritual as the only means of abolishing power, the anarchists, Godwin, Proudhon, Bakunin, Kropotkin, Stirner and Tucker, in as much as they held materialistic life conceptions, designed concrete social programs and did not recognize that spirituality must precede social change, have had their teachings reduced to conjecture, and have aptly presented the advocates of coercion with the possibility of denying anarchism's true foundations, owing to the inefficiency of the suggested means of realizing these teachings.

Sympathetic Critics

Sympathetic critics of anarchism either point out the inefficiency of the suggested means of realizing an anarchist society, the problems not responded to by such proposals or, most critically, either assume the impossibility of the goodness of humankind, the spiritual revolution, or its distance

147

and difficulty of attainment. Barrington Moore, whom we feel is a sympathetic critic, formulates his objections from the fact that federated organizational schemes contain no mechanisms either for avoiding inter-community conflict nor for preventing differential wealth among communities. He holds a view of scarcity which conceives of anarchist de-industrialization in the context of extended economic interdependence and world population expansion as having minimal potentiality.[67] He rejects the anarchist assertion that a profound transformation of "human nature" can occur within non-hierarchical life forms. Yet he believes that any future society which does not extend the historic liberal achievements will be nightmarish, as nightmarish as the continuation of what has become normal.[68] So Moore, while seriously questioning anarchism's potential for the resolution of human miseries, does not exclude the possibility of anarchism.[69]

George Bernard Shaw, commenting on the impossibilities of anarchism, indicates that anarcho-communism would require either external compulsion to labor, or else a social morality which we have failed as yet to attain. He does not deny the possibility of the final attainment of this morality but contends that the path to it lies through a transitional system which will destroy the opportunities to men of getting their living idly, and wean them from the habit of regarding such an anomaly as possible, much less honorable.[70] This argument of course promotes a transitional form of state (although not necessarily: producer's labor cards were used extensively throughout libertarian Spain and were in fact attacked by Shaw's statist friends there), but more importantly this argument rests on the assessment that anarchists are too generous in their assumptions of the goodness of human nature. Shaw feels that anarchists are too optimistic in attributing man's unsocialism to the pressures of the corrupt system under which he groans. Remove the pressure, and man will *not* think rightly, otherwise how did the corruption and oppression arise?

For Bertrand Russell, respect for the liberty of others was not a natural impulse with most men. He felt that if men's

148

actions were "wholly unchecked by external authority, we should not obtain a world in which all men would be free. The strong would oppress the weak, or the majority would oppress the more peaceable people."[71] These impulses, Russell argued, were not wholly due to a bad social system, as when new conditions of freedom obtain men easily revert to a more barbarous attitude and practice.[72] These impulses, argued Russell, could be prevented by the community but probably only through a prolonged reign of law. We have thus yet another argument against the possibility of spiritual revolution, which attempts to refute the conception of natural goodness by positing natural badness or factual badness.

OUR RESPONSE

Anarchists are acutely sensitive to the extent of man's inhumanity to man, the perpetuation of misery. *The idea of natural goodness does not mean that man does not act cruelly. It means that the extent and frequency of misery have historic variation. It means that the search is on for an explanation of these variations, both in consciousness and in social structure.* To say that man is naturally evil is to give up the search, to reconcile oneself to the current frequency and extent of misery, to interpret history and the future as lacking in substantive change, incapable of change. It is as if to say that disease is a natural phenomenon, and thus, truncate the search of medicine. "Of course disease is a natural phenomenon; but that does not alter the fact that any given disease has an assignable cause, and that if we can find the cause we may be able to cure it. You do not in the least refute that assertion by pointing to the vast extent of disease, or even by showing that the modern advances that have enabled us to cure some diseases have caused others to multiply."[73] The anarchists have made assertions about human misery similar to those Monro makes about disease. In general, no doubt, miseries are always with us, like disease; but any particular misery, like any particular disease, has specific causes, usually social ones; and it may be possible to remove them. Anarchists do not deny that the causes are far-reaching and

149

difficult to remove, but facing the journey is more vital than remaining within the confines of the state's shadows.

The searches of economists and philosophers have isolated some factors related to current economic miseries: the imperialists' requirement of crucial raw materials;[74] the marginal yet economically significant and stabilizing profit obtained through international markets and exploitation of resources;[75] the dependency on armament and waste expenditures under conditions of stagnated surplus profit markets;[76] and the cultural effects of domination, repression, and blindness to other social alternatives inherent in the primacy of technology, the ideology of science.[77] Yet, it is only this last factor which begins to address anarchist concerns with authority relations and the resulting absence of a consciousness of need for change.[78] The lack of this consciousness allows the miseries in the world to be both self- and politically imposed. It requires one to give up the search, to become self-interested, egotistical, exploitative and, circularly, to confirm humankind's inherent evilness.

To counteract this cycle, to awaken this consciousness, a spiritual awakening is necessary. For Tolstoy this spirituality is "a devout understanding of life, according to which man regards his earthly existence as only a fragmentary manifestation of the complete life, connecting his own life with infinite life, and recognizing his highest welfare in the fulfillment of the laws of this infinite life. . . . Only such a life-conception will give men the possibility . . . of combining into rational and just forms of life."[79] Tolstoy:

> "If this be so, then it is evident that it is not to the establishment of new forms that the activity of men desirous of serving their neighbor should be directed, but to the alteration and perfecting of their own characters and those of other people.
>
> "Those who act in the other way generally think that the forms of life and the character of life-conception of men may simultaneously improve. But thinking thus, they make the usual mistake of taking the result for the cause and the cause for the result or for an accompanying condition.
>
> "The alteration of the character and life-conception of men ine-

vitably brings with it the alteration of those forms in which men had lived, whereas the alteration of the forms of life not only does not contribute to the alteration of the character and life-conception of men, but, more than anything else, obstructs this alteration by directing the attention and activity of men into a false channel. To alter the forms of life, hoping thereby to alter the character and life-conception of men, is like altering in various ways the position of wet wood in a stove, believing that there can be such a position of wet fuel as will cause it to catch fire. Only dry wood will take fire independently of the position in which it is placed.

"This error is so obvious that people could not submit to it if there were not a reason which rendered them liable to it. This reason consists in this: that the alteration of the character of men must begin in themselves, and demands much struggle and labor; whereas the alteration of the forms of the life of others is attained easily without inner effort over oneself, and has the appearance of a very important and far-reaching activity."[30]

In essence, the social revolution must come from within and one must attempt to perfect self and construct with others the social institutions of this rejuvenation.[81] Tolstoy's critique of the anarchists was not so much that of their constructing social forms or recounting them historically but of others adopting these forms without spiritual revolution, or presenting these forms as set blueprints for the new order (the only acceptable, the expected social forms of organization) into which persons would fit and be transformed rather than having themselves been the social creators. Perhaps Tolstoy's reasoning indicates that the explicit social forms of the anarchists sans spirituality were yet another coercive program which would convert to a form of state. For Tolstoy, the perfection of man lies in what man is, the important thing to be, not to have.

We can accept Tolstoy's critique and stress the needed spiritual rejuvenation but this does not mean that past anarchistic life forms should not be explored, nor does it mean that futuristic contemplations, nor philosophical conceptions should not be presented. To be is not to restrict expression, to be is not to force or coerce modes on others. To paraphrase

151

Oscar Wilde: A map of the world that does not include such expression is not worth even glancing at, for it leaves out where humanity is always landing. And when humanity lands there it looks out, and seeing something better, sets sail.[82] The schemes of the anarchists have proved very practical and very threatening. They are set forth and often condemned as impractical, going against human nature. To Wilde this assessment was perfectly true. Anarchist ideas are impractical and go against human nature. But, "this is why it is worth carrying out, and that is why one proposes it. For what is a practical scheme? A practical scheme is either a scheme that is already in existence, or a scheme that could be carried out under existing conditions. But it is exactly the existing conditions that one objects to; and any scheme that could accept these conditions is wrong and foolish."[83]

Anarchism means an extended network of individuals and groups, making their own decisions, controlling their own lives, developing their individuality. Individuality means developing one's talents, not egotistically making claims on others. The social organization of these networks has been envisioned as communes, councils, syndicates, people living and working, mutually unselfishly aiding one another. The organization of work/life has been envisioned as decentralized among face to face interacting individuals who arrange their order autonomously and equally. Human society is to be arranged into a series of autonomous communities which can voluntarily form federations or links with one another. The allocation of differential resources due to climate, geography, and natural resource endowment would be shared without the currently pervasive practice or concern with extractive exchange and exploitative advantage. The criterion of being is the spirituality of connecting one's life with all life. The autonomy of one's community and one's commitment to those with whom one is in direct contact does not diminish the recognition of others' needs without this group and their essential likeness, their humanity.

To us anarchism is the moral principle of self rule, non-violence, a continuous search after perfection, personal responsibility and social welfare. Anarchism is a moral principle which engages social organizational principles. It thus engages decentralization, face-to-face communal autonomy and self-sufficiency. As a principle for organizing energy, technology and economic production and distribution, anarchism engages decentralization.

Instead of developing nuclear power, shale oil or coal gasification – modes of energy production which require centralized, capital intensive development, and are environmentally destructive[84] – solar, tidal, and wind power, accompanied by architectural innovation, are implied. To develop these modes of energy requires the decentralization of supply and distribution. Large concentrations of persons, and their energy needs, cannot be met through decentralized energy sources. Therefore, decentralized life forms must accompany non-destructive energy production and distribution.

Similarly, the economic modes of growth – giantism, complexity, capital intensive centralized control – of massive destruction, and industrialization must initiate the cessation of growth. This necessary cessation requires economic organization constructed on an accelerated work-intensive, rather than capital-intensive, basis of production.[85] The economy should be engaged by shared work rather than highly technical, energy-consumptive, worker-displacing technology. *The technology itself must be designed as non-violent, respectful of nature, of those persons who use it, and of the products.* Such an economy is obviously to be consumptively simple yet neither anti-technological nor anti-knowledge. The creation and implementation of intermediate technology[86] and knowledge must be related to the development and freedom of all persons, for each person through the dignity of their activity fulfills self and others. Work should not be a function of the isolated person, nor is the person to be an object, a manipulated factor in the means of production.

Anarchists have designed and instituted numerous constructive programs. They have projected communes, "banks," developed self-rule in agriculture, factory, community and federation.[87] They have organized peasants, wor-

153

kers, large numbers of persons, on the basis of non-violence, the hope of liberation from present and future tyranny. (Note: "The basis of non-violence" means that the basis of the structural arrangements was non-violent. We do not wish to imply that these programs and arrangements were not responded to with violence (e.g., Mexico, Ukraine, Spain) nor that the anarchists/socialists did not respond with violence in defense of their autonomy.) Yet, all these attempts recognized that institutional means could not generate a transformation of human heart. From this transformation only could the "new" society emerge. As Gandhi taught, "The spirit of sacrifice, the will and the enthusiasm of the people themselves, alone can generate any lasting change. And that will come not through power but the example of selfless service and the invitation and opportunity for people to participate in the decisions affecting their lives."[88]

SUMMARY

It can be inferred from the history of the nation-state that the ruling few have attempted to legitimate their power by claiming a higher justification for their right to rule. Concurrently, the ruled many have seldom been so docile as to not provoke such justifications. In accordance with their diverse histories, different nation-states have developed alternative state-elite managerial ideologies. In one version, the exercise of authority is justified with the assertion that the ruling few have the qualities of superiority which will enable them to realize the interests of the many. In another, authority is denied altogether on the ground that the few merely order what the many desire.

Within each managerial style there has recently developed a group of professional ideologists. Science, technology, and philosophy are harnessed to the machine; the new mandarins emerge. Universal validity is claimed for what is class, party, nation-state, or propertarian special interest. For the new mandarins, concern for human liberty, human diversity, and a just society are to be treated with scorn, as impractical or utopian. In state think-tanks the mandarins do not search for truth and justice, but program optimal operational managerial alternatives. Justice metamorphizes into universalistic treatments, equality into uniformity. All possibility for non-hierarchical forms of social life is dismissed. Obedience to hierarchy is obtained while human misery is perpetuated. Yet, many such mandarins become conscious of their own metamorphoses, and reject the state holocaust and their own objectification.

In reality, the miseries of humankind cannot simply be laid at the statehouse doors of elites or mandarins, for we, our ideas and our constructed relationships, our acceptance of hierarchy, are the state. The miseries of hunger, war, injustice, and oppression can be eliminated. And yet grievances, conflicts, disputes and unhappinesses are desirably inevitable as social life is enriched by our differences.

In essence, social revolution must come from within. One must begin by attempting to perfect self and construct with others new social institutions. And though the specific proposals of anarchists can be criticized, the nature and dignity of their inquiries and visions are unassailable.

Hoch die Anarkie

I see the poor are helped more by the poor.
My eyes weep for begger, criminal and whore.
My heart is broken by the spirits jailed;
It sinks as each freedom is assailed.

Those who toil most have the least.
They who toil not get the feast.
She is raped who steals a dollar ring.
He who steals an empire is a king.

I see four heroes swaying from the ropes;
And with them, hanging dead, their hopes;
Freedom, equality, brotherhood and future –
Lost, impossible, individuality unsure.

I see many young who remember yesteryears.
My eyes are shining with new hope – not tears.
My heart sings like the happy bird.
"Let the voice of the people (now) be heard."

Hryhori Nestor Rudenko

From Richard Rudolph, *Give Me Soil to Fly In*, (ed.) Dennis Sullivan, Baobab Books Publishers, Voorhiesville, N.Y., 1977, p. 17.

4 The Wish To Be Free: Commitment To Eden

A MATTER OF TIME

To engage the wish to be free, to search for community and freedom, we must recognize that underlying different modes of thought are assumptions about time. How time is conceived of asserts itself into what people regard as possible, how they construct their present lives, and how they struggle for authenticity. While all inquiries deal with or assume the question of time and ultimately being or presence, time within the framework of machine capitalism, and megagrowth science, is imagined and has meaning only as a straight line. Time is linear. "The present is imagined to be one point which constantly moves forward while the past consists of points to the left of the present and the future is made up of those points to the right of what is now present."[1]

This linear conception of time is drawn from mechanical models, conceived in a period of history when the motion of machines promised a glorious future through a harsh industrious present. To conceive of time in this manner is to limit one's conception of valuable experience to the scientific, a critically limited model of life, for it is to view time as outside human events. The linear image places human experience into the realm of the abstract. There is no presence in space for there are no present relationships to others; one's person is always absent! The linear image collapses human history and human experience. It reduces human expression to a mechanistic, superficial, lifeless level. To accept this conception is ultimately to choose against the human struggle, to deny its validity.

Accepting the linear model means accepting the reality that, as the line never ends, so too one can never "attain" or

157

"be." Happiness and freedom are never a present reality and, therefore, one is never free from the fate of what might happen. Happiness and freedom are always a set of experiences that will occur, but that always manage to avoid the present. It is a set of experiences that requires constant dissatisfaction with the present, that suggests that the present cannot be altered or changed only ever so slightly in the causal chain of progress. "So heavily are we laden with the debris of the past," Bookchin writes, "and so pregnant are we with the possibilities of the future that our estrangement with the world reaches the point of anguish."[2] The realization of oneself as creator, as poet, as artist who need not destroy to be, to exist, to create, to be satisfied remains at the level of fantasy. There is in fact *never time for it*!

In contrast to this mechanical model of time is the choice to make the present paramount. To be human, to be sensitive to what is innermost in one's person and in others, is to be present, not to be futured or basing one's presence on future possibilities, which while they may actualize, always do so at a time other than now. Only in the present does the struggle to be human exist; only in the present is there the possibility to be human. To think in terms of the past or future is to think outside the present and to escape from the human situation. (The focus on the present is of course linked to past biography and future social existence. A non-linear conception of time and a social, collective sense of future means that we must preserve the earth's environment for all who follow and act in the interests of all our children and theirs to come.)

Many of us have become obsessed with the way things were or with how they might be, bypassing the present and the possibility of engaging in relationships of care. We essentially turn ourselves outside space!

We have been obsessed with the future to the point where future possibilities "ensure" being present in the future. But being absent now means that community is not now possible, for relationships of care are not possible now. That many in our society speak of "future shock" is revealing for the future is shocking only when the present is shocking, when there is no worthwhile present to speak of, when the present is given little value.

A greater focus on the present represents not merely a shift from one point in time to another (time has no points) but an altered state of mind affecting interior-exterior relationships. In the present one constructs, relates, acts and *is*; now is real, and meaningful. The future is unknown and elusive as it will always be. What matters is the quality of life in the present. We cannot accept the presence of dominance, external authority or hierarchy and their promises of future betterment, liberty and freedom from authority. To be present is to reject instruments external to human experience. External authority and hierarchy as exhibited in capitalist and party dictatorship state institutions reinforce relationships in the abstract and suppress the power to be present to self and others. Community, a life of present sharing through relationship, is never a possibility within such arrangements.

Clearly, at times, it is necessary to represent events historically. It is, however, neither necessary to describe nor necessary to experience human events with a linear, future-progress or scientific model. Through a linear model, an attempt is made to efface time; in the name of progress the human being is eventually undercut.[3] Yet, in the context of community, there is a choice to be present to experience, to be present to those who care enough to be present to us and to renew that presence. Within such a context, any question of "deviance" is no longer individualistic, but stands within an ethic of shared meaning and collective responsibility, for all are responsible for present events and their creation. A shared experience through shared presence generates care; a shared presence gives meaning to an ethic of shared responsibility. Authority to "enforce" exists only insofar as the authority to be present exists and continues. There is no "enforcement" required in being present, for the power of self in acts of creation, in the act of being present is more powerful and contains more meaning for persons than any external force or institutional arrangement. The power of community, of collective presence extends far beyond hierarchy or "enforcement" and renders it unnecessary.

People within community can immerse themselves into mutually dependent, personal and collective history and project it into the future, for the present is meaningful, happy and secure. They can find meaning in the past, for the past is constructed in the present and can project possibilities for the future. (When we say the past is constructed in the present, we mean that past experiences are interpreted, constructed, and take their meaning in terms of the present relationships that people have.) It is only when the present is not secure or meaningful (in time) that there is movement toward the past or toward the future, over which hierarchy moves to control. The present celebrates with peculiar intensity "the moments in which the past reinforces the present and in which the future is a quickening of what is now."[4]

Human creativity flows from human experience. In the present we experience and are sensitive to what is present to our senses. We do not experience a given act, feeling or thought in terms of what has gone before but experience the act, feeling or thought as it reveals itself in the present. In the present, we can escape external programing which constrains us and makes us a passive component of experience. John Cage has described this experience in music as the need to listen to what is there, to be sensitive to what is present to the ears, to not listen to a given note in terms of what has gone before, but to listen to the musical piece as it reveals itself in the present. The present is thus a time for action, for making music, for entering and being part of the creative process. It is a freeing experience for the person, it is a freeing of the ecology of the person to its natural components. It is the recognition that personal environments do not have to be destroyed for persons as artists to create.

THE HISTORY OF HUMANKIND: THE LINEAR-PROGRESS, MODERNIZATION PERSPECTIVE

The history of humankind presented in the social sciences is often one of unilinear progress. Historical forces are believed

160

to have provided the political, economic and psychological basis for an expansion of freedom and autonomy. Only through slow progress, modernization and significant rational control of affect have freedom and personal autonomy become possible. Personal autonomy becomes the power to identify and choose among the object world, rationally and independently of the inconsistencies of intuition and historically defined myths of authority.

In this progressive rationalization account, the most powerful sources of discontent and social action (revolution) have been: (1) the demand for *autonomy* from authority – political, economic, religious, and finally psychic; (2) the demand for *inclusion* on all institutional levels; and (3) the conflict arising from opposing wishes to extend or limit the bases of inclusion in society.[5] Weinstein and Platt suggest that:

> "The organization of institutional (market) structures within which the highly complex and demanding autonomous activities could be sustained – on the necessary basis of self discipline, rationality and the withdrawal of affect – legitimated the public expression of a high degree of aggressive behavior. The need to display constantly a compulsive, "masculine" activity and the ability to define others as incapable of this activity provided the psychic basis for exploitative relationships. This negative consequence, however, has overshadowed the positive contribution of the movement toward autonomy, which was to separate the individual from authority (from passive, submissive commitments to important figures of the past), so that objects and actions could be evaluated with some degree of independent control. This is the crucial test of all revolutionary activity, for freedom has no meaning if it is not the freedom to choose the objects that one is to be related to, and this becomes possible only after dependent connections to authority are severed."[6]

The progress-rationalization account conceives the historical contribution of the middle class as neither their productive facilities nor their commitment to rationality, but rather the vital break with authority on all levels of activity (religion, political, economic, family). This break, it is postulated, was made by the creation of and through the develop-

161

ment of abstract relationships, a situation whereby authority could be dealt with in some independent way, namely through the development of written legal codes and bureaucratic formal regulations. These become the means for achieving the desired degrees of freedom. Revolutionary attempts to become free of economic exploitation by seizing control of both economic and political institutions are treated as historically impossible. Similarly, revolutionary attempts to become free of economic exploitation and political hierarchy are treated as historically absent. As freedom is only a futured wish or dream for the progressive and rational, there can be no place for believers in the present, nor credence given to their existence or struggles. The progressive-modernization account is summarized as follows by Weinstein and Platt:

> "The attempt to deal with the problems of aggression, conflict, and exploitation on the basis of authoritarian control over economic and political institutions was bound to end with regressive social forms because the identifications and internalizations necessary for the support of autonomous activity did not exist, and control over a chaotic internal and external situation of revolutionary change could only be achieved by the systematic use of violence. Further, authority relationships had still to be predicated on the traditional passivity, dependence, and subordination. However, any evolution toward higher levels of social existence must be based on the termination of traditional commitments to authority and, above all, this is what the middle class achieved in the modern era."[7]

The history of humankind from this perspective presents relationships to authority as having "evolved from a pre-oedipal emphasis on passivity and dependence to an oedipal emphasis on competitive autonomy – a position that is based to a significant degree on the rational control of affect."[8] Progress has been made, they say. With further social structural change these current relationships to authority will continue to evolve in a "fraternal" direction with less emphasis on agressive competition and more emphasis on affectual commitments.[9] Again and again, freedom from authority is "futured," life is qualitatively evolving for the better. The irony here is that persons are always expected to *become* free, and to *become* human some place else and some time else. In reality, in the present all become placeless and timeless. The relative and finite characteristics of the human are rejected, which ultimately supports defining the human out of the human, and preserving freedom as a wish and not a present reality.

THE HISTORY OF HUMANKIND: A CRITIQUE OF THE LINEAR PERSPECTIVE

Even in the evidence supportive of the progress model of human history, the unilinear model is contradicted. In the Weinstein and Platt argument, for example, exploitative relationships have dominated the movement toward autonomy. For some critics of the human progress account the central fact of recent history is that freedom and personal autonomy have become more precarious than ever before. According to Lash, the same historical forces that have provided the political, economic and psychological basis of an unprecedented expansion of freedom and autonomy are now engaged in their very subversion.[10] We are coming to realize, however obliquely, that while human progress may be limitless, the role of conqueror and exploiter of nature is definitely limited.[11] Lash argues:

"No longer able to turn its back on the psychic devastation that surrounds us, as it formally attempted to do, social science explains it away as the price of progress. It attributes the symptoms of a new psychic enslavement to freedom. It dignifies chaos as 'pluralism', moral collapse as an expansion of 'personal choice', narcissism as autonomy. In this way it attempts to assure itself and its readers that modernization is proceeding on schedule."[12]

In contrast to the progress-modernization account of history, Lash feels that the really significant factor in the historical development of autonomy was the emotional inten-

163

sification of family life in the bourgeois family, which strengthened the child's identification with his or her parents. "This at once sharpened the struggle necessary to achieve autonomy and gave it a stronger basis by forcing the individual to develop inner resources instead of relying on external direction."[13] But as the family changed in its relations to the outside world, the psychic costs of this intense socialization increased. The family became a refuge, a private retreat, the center of a new kind of emotional-affectual life, a new intimacy and inwardness. Lash states that:

> "From the moment the conception of the family as a refuge made its historical appearance, the same forces that gave rise to the new privacy began to erode it. The nineteenth century cult of the home, where the woman ministered to her exhausted husband, repaired the spiritual damage inflicted by the market, and sheltered her children from its corrupting influence, expressed the hope on which bourgeois society has always rested – that the private satisfactions can compensate for deprivations suffered in the realm of work. But the machinery of organized domination, which had impoverished work and reduced civic life to a competitive free-for-all, soon organized 'leisure' itself as an industry. The so-called privatization of experience went hand in hand with an unprecedented assault on privacy. The tension between the family and the economic and political order, which in the early stages of bourgeois society had protected the members of the family from the full impact of the market, gradually abated."[14]

With respect to most children, the present situation is qualitatively no different:

> "Today the peer group introduces the child to the illusory delights of consumption at an early age, and the family, drained of the emotional intensity that formally characterized domestic relations, socializes him into the easygoing, low-keyed relationships that predominate in the outside world as well. Capitalism in its advanced stages has reduced conflict between society and the family to a minimum. Whereas in earlier times the family passed on the dominant values but unavoidably provided the child with a glimpse of a world that transcended them, crystalized in the

rich imagery of maternal love, capitalism has now eliminated or at least softened this contradiction. The family, assisted by the health industry, the mass media, the monolithic national culture, and its mirror image the counterculture, produces a type of personality primed not for 'achievement,' as the Parsonians would have it, but for immediate instinctual gratification – the perfect consumer, in short."[15]

Not only is the current bourgeois child the consumed consumer, but for most, the wish to be free, the expansion of autonomy and choice is limited to consumptive narcissism, not exclusively of materials but of persons as well. One survives and has value by passing through the materials and persons defined as part of the object world, of the world out there, of the world without affect. One's inner self, one's sense of value is equated with one's status to consume. If, as the linear progressive rationalists assume, progress continues on the basis of suppressing affect, emotion and expressive feelings, then the foundation of life, evolution, history and progressive good, is the process of differentiation and suppression. Suppression becomes the hub of the historical progress of humankind!

If, as the linear progressive rationalists assume, the history of humankind evolves on the basis of suppressing affect, emotion, and expressive feelings, then progress, the wish to be free, autonomy from authority and social action is a "male" endeavor. The progress of history is male history! The history of humankind is the history of the differentiation of males from females; of differentiating rationality-instrumentality from emotionality-expressive affect. The successful revolution of humankind requires suppression: males suppressing females; males suppressing themselves, their feelings and emotions; females suppressing their rationality; all drowning under hierarchical suppression. By this account, present and ongoing suppression, hierarchy and authority are supported as necessary to the *future* freedom of humankind. The rationalists support suppression *now*! No person is considered whole! The contest continues for the next generation of fittest!

This critical uncovering of the linear rationalists' account of human history is even further supported by their concept of the demand for inclusion. The wish to be free, the demand for autonomy, is always accompanied by the demand for inclusion. However, inclusion does not mean social relatedness and a greater sense of unity and mutuality. It means the demand for participation in hierarchical authority, in dominance, in suppressive hierarchical relationships and structures.

This conception of inclusion is critical to maintaining rationalist commitment to the consensual model of social and political life. What is designated as "revolution" is political action which extends the degree of inclusion, participation or enfranchisement for larger numbers of persons or categories of persons. If this extension has occurred historically, an issue debated amongst pluralists and elite scholars, these actions are indeed *political* and not *social* (actions) revolutions. They are in fact counter-revolutionary, for they reject the social. They are mere changes in the form or image of the authoritarian state.

An historical account of the French "revolution" is often offered as an example of the extension of inclusion. But the French social revolution is always edited out of existence. The concomitant personal and social revolution of the many persons who formed the Paris Commune is historically slighted or altogether neglected. Similarly, in the historical accounts of the Russian "revolutions" only the political revolution, the second revolution, is presented. The revolutions of large numbers of persons and their created revolutionary social structures are discounted. The history of the Makhnovists, for example, is dismissed or not recounted. The accounts for Spain are equally distorted.

The wish to be free from authority and included in authority, the wish to be free from suppression and to be included in suppression is not merely contradictory and paradoxical, but has served to intellectualize and support hierarchical authority and its suppression of the present life, now, while promising slow progress toward freedom in the future.[16] We have, they say, neither the knowledge nor introspection necessary to be free, to create a social order free of hierarchical authority. They claim that the choice not to be included in hierarchy, not to enter the power struggle, is a wish for an imagined past, for dependence and simplicity. It seems even questionable whether the rationalist-inclusionists can conceive of a social order for whole persons, who suppress neither self (rationality or emotionality) nor others. They most certainly do not wish for such a social order. Weinstein and Platt:

> "It remains a fundamental error of utopians to imagine that the just or decent society must or will be a simple one, to hope that social structures will not inevitably lead to some degree of anxiety, or to assume that psychic support for the tolerance of social demands will follow virtually automatically from some planned reorganization of productive and distributive networks. Moreover, those critics of modern societies who view complexity as some kind of deception, repudiate superego and ego oriented abstract and instrumental relationships, and insist that an end to separation and reestablishment of expressive attachments on all levels are both necessary and possible – those critics misconstrue what can be achieved, given the present level of control over psychic and social structures. The desire to organize a 'community' beyond the possibility for struggle or the existence of aggression is not an objectively based aspiration and is not indicative of what is available for the future; rather, it is a wish that relates to the past – the dependent past. We have, in fact, little knowledge of or control over object relations, or, more specifically, over unconscious materials, and it is difficult to say what combination of psychic and social structural conditions would be likely to produce significant degrees of such knowledge and control. But without these conditions, the hoped-for expressive commitments cannot lead to increased personal freedom; they must tend rather to the re-establishment of subordinate relationships based on the uncritical acceptance of nurturant and protective figures."[17]

Weinstein and Platt argue curiously and quite correctly that "modern (political) revolutionary movements that have intervened in economic and political processes on the assumptions that: (1) the dominant source of anxiety and aggression lies in the productive sphere of endeavor; and that (2) control over the economic and political machinery would

167

lead to control over human nature; have failed to realize their primary goal, which was precisely a fundamental change in individual motivation. The 'planned' authoritarian control over economic and political processes has not led to conscious control over psychic and social structures. . . ."[18] Of course it has not! *Hierarchical authority, in all its various forms of suppression, demands dependence, passivity and subordination.* However, ironically, because its process is suppressive it generates resistance – the wish to be free. It could thus be concluded from these arguments that both liberative and repressive tensions or ends are generated from hierarchical historical "progress." But, in reality there are no ends, only process.[19] And process is *now*. Each means must *now* correspond with what one substantively desires. *Each process and means, must now, in the present, be justifiable.*

If authority, hierarchical, external and rational, is to be replaced, it must happen by the very process in which persons acquire power over their own lives, in which persons "discover" themselves, their natural relationships to others through mutual aid, and in which they experience the power to be present to self and others in the context of community. Personal and social revolutions occur only in the present, as a continuous process. Therefore, to speak of revolution or freedom as an "end product" is to use language that resides outside human experience, outside the context of experienced organic living arrangements. It implies a deliverer, someone or some process outside the authenticity of the human experiences of the community who/which will liberate. Social as well as personal revolutions evolve from the "organics" of the human, not from futuristic metaphysical promises. The actions of persons in community who are present to their own realities speak freedom and revolution. The meaning of life must be found in human experience.

THE SEARCH FOR COMMUNITY: UTOPIA

The search for community, for meaning in life and an appreciation of human experience in the present, requires *the reality,*

168

not the wish, to be free of authority. Freedom in the present is antithetical to both the rationalist-inclusionist account and to support for authoritarian "progress." It is also antithetical to any search for utopia.

The utopian search for community and alternative life-styles is now presented in the media as descriptive of a resurgence of interest in community – communalism – mutual aid. However, utopias past and present, while popularly given positive value as a search for community are often a search for passivity, dependence, and submission to authority.[20] They are an exchange of one total institution for another. Utopias were and are, often, the personal searches of charismatic individuals to control others, to provide systems of pre-planned lifestyles wherein to escape from life's struggles and contradictions. Correspondingly, utopias were and are, often, the personal searches of many individuals to be passively and dependently secure, to be subordinate to authority, to be smothered notwithstanding an alternative reality.

Though the utopian ethic is very similar to the corporate ethic which the media uphold, utopian searches for community are criticized in the media as impractical and escapist from our megamachine culture. Indeed, the authoritarian communes of the counter-culture while offering relief from the megamachine economy offer little relief from the mega-hierarchy of authority. While individuals may temporarily resolve personal dilemmas and contradictions in the lap of communal authoritarianism, it is no less true that the resolution of the issue of autonomy, to be free of authority, is not offered. Mumford comments:

> "Strangely, though the word freedom is sometimes included in the descriptions of utopia . . . the pervasive character of all utopias is their totalitarian absolutism, the reduction of variety and choice, and the effort to escape from such natural conditions of historical traditions as would support variety and make choice possible. These uniformities and compulsions constitute utopia's inner tie to the megamachine."[21]

In the context of authoritarian utopia, the concept of commitment has come to mean the willingness of persons to give their energy and loyalty to the social system such that each person through personal introspective thought attaches him or her self to social relations which are seen as self-expressive.[22] The social system itself, according to Kanter, has specific problems which may be met through social arrangements or social mechanisms which involve and bind persons to the communal order. These system problems can possibly be met or satisfied through a variety of types of commitment, each of which engages a different personality system component (for example cognitive, cathetic, relational – illustrated below).

The critical social system problem of any communal order is survival. Giving a commitment to participate (continuation commitment) involves each person's *cognitive* evaluation. Consequently, most continuing communal utopias have required members to invest in and sacrifice to the commune. Each person is often required to invest his or her present and potential future resources to the community. Each person is, as well, often required to sacrifice – to practice abstinence or austerity. Such mechanisms make continuing membership costly and/or sacred, increase one's commitment to utopia and rationally commit each to comply with the *roles* of the utopian order.

The problem of cohesiveness is almost as critical to the utopian social order as the problem of survival. Surviving utopian communities, those which have survived for considerable periods of time, have developed mechanisms which elicit each member's *cathetic* (emotional) commitment to the others. In order to survive, they have often required members to relinquish all *relational* attachments such that a monopoly of affective ties is contained within the commune. Boundaries or barriers separating the community from the external world are often clearly developed both relationally and spatially. Similarly, within the commune affective ties are sharply curtailed except those to the synergic whole, the one-ness of the group. Dyadic and family relations are often renounced. Furthermore, renounced competing ties are often complemented by the processes of communion whereby each, through sharing property, labor, food and spiritual celebrations, relinquishes self-separateness in order to identify with collective consciousness.

The problem of control is another mutually dependent utopian order problem. Social control issues are those which involve each person's *evaluative* attachment to uphold communal beliefs, norms and authority as correct, moral, just, legitimate and as expressing one's own values. Social mechanisms are often developed to induce each person to see him or her self as carrying out the dictates of a higher *moral system,* which orders and gives meaning to life. Through mortification and surrender, the individual exchanges private identity for one provided by the "social order." Identity becomes anchored in communal actions, meaning comes from ideology, institutionalized awe, hierarchy and de-individuating mechanisms which mortify the individual, show him or her to be small before the great whole and test his or her faith and commitment to the utopian, authoritarian order.[23]

Attempts at utopia are oriented toward continuance of the communal order, its structure. To further this continuance and to realize utopian ideals, members are enmeshed in mechanisms programed to elicit commitment. The function of this commitment is to serve the commune's needs, its messianic mission, its survival and to subordinate individual needs. Yet many people have been and can be joyous losing their individuality in the utopian commune. The utopian tradition can develop a stable harmonious society of persons who defer to the common good, or alternatively produce one of passive, dependent persons moved mechanistically by totalitarian authority.[24] Regardless, in no way does the search for utopia either continue the thrust of the wish for autonomy or its present realization. Rather, it extends the wish for social and psychic inclusion and dependence on authority.

THE SEARCH FOR COMMUNITY: EDEN

There are available other traditions and accounts of the wish

171

to be free and the history of humankind. In contrast to the utopian and rational-inclusionist traditions, the wish to be free is currently visible in a resurgence of the search for community which is not a search for utopia. The thrust of this tradition is away from the planned social order and towards what is imagined to be a blessed state of nature, an effort to regain Eden[25] through personal creativity, self autonomy, primitive delight and sociality. Members of edenistic communities are committed to developing self-reliance, self-realization and as well mutual aid, concern and trust.

Each of us surely recognizes that all persons have an individualistic tendency. This tendency increases the intensity, joy, and meaningfulness of life. Yet the survival of humankind has been, the predominant fact of nature has been, *mutual aid*. The survival of humankind has been based in cooperation, mutual support, the imagination and extension of self which Shelley so poignantly described:

> "The great secret of morals is love: or a going out of our own nature, and an identification of ourselves with the beautiful which exists in thought, action, or person, not our own. A man, to be greatly good, must imagine intensely and comprehensively; he must put himself in the place of another and of many others; the pains and pleasures of his species must become his own."[26]

Like nature's symbiotic balances, the balance between humankind's individualistic tendency (egoism) and utopian immersion (suppression), as well, is found in each human being. There is no real conflict between the individual and social tendencies; the one is the receptacle of a precious life essence, the other is the repository of the element that keeps the essence pure and strong. "The individual is the heart of society, conserving the essence of social life; society is the lungs which are distributing the element to keep the life essence – that is, the individual – pure and strong."[27] *The conception of self and forms of commitment in edenistic communities encourage, not narcissistic selfishness, but the discovery that the more conscious one is of being bound to others and to nature, the freer one is to be unique, different and autonomous.* "To be linked is to be

172

whole."[28] The more one is conscious of the seriousness of being present, the greater the exaltation of being free.

In contradiction to the utopian commitments to continuance and survival of the messianic social order, edenistic commitment is *not* to structure. Edenistic commitment is to autonomy, mutual dependence, and the belief in organic freedom – the unity of humankind in nature. Judson Jerome states:

> "In an organic view of life the natural impulse of people is to grow, change, to rectify error as a stalk seeks sunlight, to seek self-actualization through symbiotic relationships with other self-actualizing and very diverse individuals (as healthy flowers require healthy bees, and vice versa). Mechanistic controls and constraints interrupt this process. Conformity, or repression of self, results from surrendering inner motives to external expectations. A farmer does not 'grow' (an odd verb in the transitive, as is 'heal') his corn by stretching it on a rack, but by fertilizing its roots and clearing the way for it to develop. Given the right conditions an ecosystem will establish itself as a heterogeneous plentitude in which each component thrives."[29]

The commitment to Eden is not a commitment to a specific group of persons, a specific set social order. It is a commitment to relationships with individual equals, a grouping which knows no borders, no walls. Persons so committed are free, for they have something to live for, have someone to live with. They can engage in the present. Persons so related of course are present to specific groups and federations at any given time, but such persons are disseminated throughout the natural world. Persons so committed like those of Black Mountain[30] flow in life's stream, moved, energized by freedom from authority, constrained not, still loving and still loved.

The communities of such persons neither cease to exist, nor become "unsuccessful" attempts at community when they disperse. The commitment of such persons is to autonomy and mutual dependence – a unity. Dependence in edenistic culture is neither the wish for inclusion in hierarchical authority nor the wish to be dependent on or subject to such authority. It is rather to share responsibility for relations with others and the direction of one's life; to be mutually aided and aiding. Jerome argues:

"Nature, except for humankind, lives in anarchy. Not lawlessly, of course; indeed, it seems that only humankind can violate its implacable laws. But in that environment which we despoil and from which we so desperately shield ourselves, there are no constitutions or hierarchies, no officials, no roles (that world is not a stage), no schedules, no duties – though there are imperative loyalties requiring the mother tirelessly to feed her young, the mate to defend the bower, the species to maintain itself, even by stratagems as destructive to individuals as lemming migrations. In that anarchy, tragedy is linked to bounty irrevocably as winter to autumn, and affirmation to negation with the mindless persistence of March shoots pushing through rotten snow. In political terms anarchy means the abnegation of power, but that belies the reality. Rather it is adoption of the greatest power available, riding the wave of nature's dynamics, identifying with insuperable forces. 'Politics,' Buckminster Fuller once said, 'is of the machine age, obsolete.' If we can find a way to unleash the new anarchism, with its promise not of chaos but of the supreme orderliness and dependable rhythm of nature, it will make politics unthinkable as warfare is made by the possibility of nuclear holocaust.

"Finding a way to unleash it is a slow, sensitive task, like that of bank thieves with sanded fingers sensing the muted fall of tumblers that lock in the mystery. A paradigm for the task is the lesson of love. If I desire you, I must recognize that sexual pressure may be exactly what will drive you away. If I love *you* and not a reflection of myself, I must want you to be what you are, not shape you to my wishes. That may mean I must learn to be glad if you love another, if you choose to leave me. And those hard lessons must be learned in the midst of intense passion, not through diminishment of feeling, but through its increase, by learning to care enough not to destroy.

"The world beyond the looking glass will seem much like the one we leave – or at least the one on blueprints produced by humane intelligence. Only the motives will be reversed, and the fruit looking just like perfectly manufactured wax will, strangely, be real, edible, perishable. The factory will run – without pressure, without wages, its profits absorbed by the community as

174

unceremoniously and uncompetitively as air is breathed and water drunk. People will make pots as they prepare and eat a meal, sleep, make love, sweat, defecate – as something that must be done, that one can learn to like to do.

"Or so we hope. For those of us who have lived long on the wrong side of the glass, adjustment to the reversed world will no doubt always be somewhat self-conscious and awkward, like immigrants who even after many years in their new home still dream and count in the old language."[31]

THE ECONOMICS OF EDEN: THE STRUGGLE TO BE HUMAN

The basic economic tenets of edenistic culture are: (1) re-assessing needs; (2) doing more with less; and (3) the belief that nature is essentially good, as is humankind as part of nature. "The welfare of one species depends upon the welfare of all others in its environment, even that of its natural enemies."[32] While the "rational" economic domination of the earth, of nature, of all species, for profit has been the practice of death dealing and life degeneration, the consciousness of organic ecology, in contrast, enables all species to live in an environment without destroying either them or it.

The linear-progress account of human history and linear reactions contradicting it have dichotomized the experience of whole human life. In much the same way that sexes, races, and species have been dichotomized and pitted against each other, rationality has been pitted against affect. The separation of knowledge-rationality and its promise of future freedom from feeling, aid, and affect and their independent promise of freedom is a dichotomous insensitivity to organic thought, the wholeness of human life. It has led us to a mechanistic detachment from basic human qualities. Science and reason have been isolated and reified as separate from poetry, affect and imagination. One or the other has been evidenced as contributing and/or detracting from the pres-ence of freedom. Shelley, for example, while acknowledging that reasoners and mechanics had had their utility in the

banishment of want, the security of life, the dispersal of superstition, and the conciliation of interests, felt that poetry and
imagination were of equal if not greater utility.[33] Reinhard
Bendix relates that for Shelley:

"The great difficulty is that in scientific and economic systems of
thought 'the poetry . . . is concealed by the accumulation of facts
and calculating processes.' Certainly, the sciences have enlarged
our 'empire over the external world.' But in proportion as the
poetic faculty is wanting, the sciences have also circumscribed the
empire of the internal world.[34] Shelley continues: 'We want the
creative faculty to imagine that which we know; . . . (but) our cal-
culations have outrun our conception; we have eaten more than
we can digest. . . . The cultivation of poetry is never more to be
desired than at periods when . . . the accumulation of the materials of external life exceeds . . . the power of assimilating them
to the internal laws of human nature.'[35]"[36]

An organic conception of humanness can reject neither
technology-rationality nor poetry-affect. To do so would be to
count on suppressive analytical processes to emancipate a
fantasy. According to Murray Bookchin, the scarcity model of
economics is no longer applicable because of the mega- and
medium technology we have developed. The new technology
– doing more with less – especially on an energy economics
base, "makes possible a miniaturization, decentralization,
and diversification which could reverse the tendency of earlier
technology to gigantize, amalgamate and standardize."[37]
(Note: Though we support miniaturization, decentralization,
and diversification we are not against voluntary-linked technology between communities such as rail transportation.
Furthermore, our argument should not be construed to be
pro-privatization. We are for collective-mutual community
tools owned by no one person and accessible to all.) Modes of
thought dependent on the premise of scarcity of necessary resources are now uneconomic,[38] as well as dysfunctional in
accomodating humankind to its present and future. Jerome:

"Human association in the new era must be pervaded by spiritual awareness – of the sacredness of self, others, the environ-

176

ment, the cosmos. Material abundance not only does not exist now for most of the people on earth, but it has become clear that the planet cannot bear such abundance unless there is a radical revision of what is rapidly becoming a universal standard of material welfare. We are stripping the earth to pour goods into the bottomless maw of consumerism, creating hordes seething with envy and pustules of glut. There remains an incompleted task of providing adequate food, clothing, shelter, medical care, education, and amenities for the world population; but this has been confused with the endless process of arousing and catering to artifically created appetites. We suffer more seriously from a spiritual malaise, a problem of values, than from a problem of economics or government or technical ability. In my view, that is the meaning of post-scarcity: we have ventured to the point that we know we could supply, until resources are exhausted and the earth is polluted beyond redemption, material goods for human-kind, and can see that the demand will be forever unsatisfied. Post-scarcity does not mean that scarcities have been or can be eliminated; it means that we can now see that we have to stop thinking in quantitative terms about human needs, or, better, cir-cumscribe our ambitions for quantitative increase by recognizing our qualitative needs."[39]

Utilizing middle range, human-intensive, technological rationality revives the spirituality of connectedness, mutual dependence, and mutual autonomy. The natural technology of Schumacher and Fuller is oriented toward self-sufficient, decentralized, life economics which involve experiencing nature. Rationality cannot be pitted against creativity and affect, for they are mutually dependent aspects of each of us. With organic economics, this technology-spirituality, it is possible for autonomous communities to flourish and link with no courts, no laws, no idea or institution of state to con-strict the commitments and autonomy of individuals and communities.

FREEDOM: THE STRUGGLE TO BE HUMAN

Within an environment of natural economics, the struggle to be human is energized and becomes an exuberant expansion of life.[40] It is here that the active forces are found through which wholly developed individuals, who have struggled to perfect their own nature, can concomitantly act to energize the whole of humankind. From the process of the struggle to perfect self, the overflow of energy spreads one's intelligence, love and energy of action to others.[41] Nature's solidarity, symbiosis and mutual aid translated into the sphere of humankind requires equity, egalitarian self-restraint, and more.

The struggle to be human requires more than exercising the principle of equity as a base for justice. It requires more than treating others as you would like them to treat you under similar circumstances.[42] It requires more than not wanting to be ruled, and therefore not ruling others. It requires more than feeding the hungry, as one knows hunger's ache. It requires being present to one's life work and others in caring relationships. It requires us to demonstrate our struggling new consciousness, to energize others with our exuberance, to develop new relationships and attempt to be pure and strong.

Self-reciprocity and mutual aid are processes which energize a social order in which *equity* is only the minimal principle of association. The struggle to be human inspires a love for others which goes far beyond the requirements of justice.[43] The struggle to be human unwaveringly shows freedom to be infinite and unbounded. Bakunin:

> "It is untrue that the freedom of the individual is bounded by that of any other individual. Man is truly free only to the extent that his own freedom, freely acknowledged and reflected as in a mirror by the free conscience of all other men, finds in their freedom the confirmation of its infinite scope."[44]

Boundless freedom in our commitment to Eden means not only that one is truly free only among equally free persons, but as well that the liberty of each person can therefore be realized only by the equality of all. The equality is non-imposition, non-invasion, self-regulation and mutual aid. By equality we do not mean that one could have equal relations with any set of two or more persons. This is impossible as each person is unique. The equity is that one does equally not

178

bound any other person. Boundless freedom is the consciousness and demonstration of the unity of life, the unity of humankind in nature. Emma Goldman:

"It is not a negative thing of being free from something, because with such freedom you may starve to death. Real freedom, true liberty, is positive: It is freedom to something; it is the liberty to be, to do; in short, the liberty of actual and active opportunity"[45] . . . "to choose the mode of work, the conditions of work, and the freedom to work. . . . The making of a table, the building of a home, or the tilling of the soil . . . [should be] what the painting is to the artist and the discovery to the scientist – the result of inspiration, of intense longing and deep interest in work as a creative force."[46]

Freedom to be, to be a creative force means to act without authority, without imposing one's own will on others. It means that each person who has the creative force to develop specific skills and understandings succeeds in affecting others by his or her actions and creativity. It means that social organization without authority accepts the inevitable and beneficial fact of human uniqueness and diversity, encourages it, survives from its mutual dependence.

Within an environment of such freedom and social organization, anti-person, anti-nature, and anti-social acts need not be feared. Each and all are energized by the acceptance of his or her individuality, skills, talents, understandings, energy, and by the acceptance of mutual aid as a human and natural principle. Such an environment, such a presence of freedom, as a process, requires a continuous struggle to be human. We must therefore be free from any idea of freedom as an end, as a state.[47] Freedom so conceived has no limits nor can it be anchored in a program for the future which ends the struggle. Inseparable from the tyranny of hierarchy and authority, the wish to be free, the struggle to become free, now, continues.

179

Notes

INTRODUCTION:
THE STRUGGLE TO BE HUMAN

1 Loren Eiseley, *Invisible Pyramid*, Scribner, New York, 1972, p. 146.
2 Jacob Bronowski, *Science and Human Values*, Harper-Row, New York, 1956.
3 Alvin Gouldner, *The Coming Crisis of Western Sociology*, Basic, New York, 1970, p. 41.
4 Gerald Runkle, *Anarchism Old and New*, Delecorte, New York, 1972, p. 281.
5 Jean-Paul Sartre, *Being and Nothingness: An Essay on Phenomenological Ontology*, Philosophical Library, New York, 1956, pp. 439, 483.
6 Alexander Berkman, *Now and After: ABC of Communist Anarchism*, Vanguard, New York, 1929, p. 180.
7 Sartre, *op.cit.*, p. 483.
8 Berkman, *op.cit.*, p. 180.
9 *Ibid.*, p. 179.
10 *Ibid.*, p. 28.
11 Jonathan Kozol, *The Night is Dark and I am Far From Home*, Houghton Mifflin, Boston, 1975, p. 14.
12 *Ibid.*, p. 12.
13 Anthony Platt, "Prospects for a Radical Criminology in the United States," *Crime and Social Justice*, 1, Spring-Summer 1974, p. 7.
14 Alfred McClung Lee, "On the Fate of Humanism in Social Science," *SSSP Social Problems Theory Division Newsletter*, no. 5, winter 1976, pp. 18–19.
15 Gabriel Moran, *The Present Revelation: In Quest of Religious Foundations*, Seabury, New York, 1972, p. 10.
16 William James as quoted in William Braden, *The Private Sea: LSD and the Search for God*, Quadrangle, Chicago, 1967, p. 31.

180

17 Issac D. Balbus, "The Concept of Interest in Pluralist and Marxist Analysis," *Politics and Society*, Feb. 1971, p. 3.

18 American Friends Service Committee, *Struggle for Justice: A Report on Crime and Punishment in America*, Hill & Wang, New York, 1971, p. 102.

19 Lewis Mumford, *The Pentagon of Power*, Harcourt Brace Jovanovich, New York, 1970, p. 429.

20 Moran, *op. cit.*

21 Martin Heidegger, *An Introduction to Metaphysics*, trans. Ralph Manheim, Yale University Press, New Haven, 1959.

22 Lynn White, *Machina Ex Deo: Essays in the Dimensions of Western Culture*, M.I.T. Press, Cambridge, 1968, p. 84.

23 Alan Watts, *Does It Matter?*, Vintage, New York, 1971, p. xiv.

24 Mumford, *op. cit.*, p. 57, makes a critique of Galileo in essentially the same language.

25 *Ibid.*, p. 430.

26 Platt, *op.cit.*, p. 3.

27 David Matza, *Becoming Deviant*, Prentice-Hall, Englewood Cliffs, N. J., 1969.

28 James T. Carey, *Sociology and Public Affairs: The Chicago School*, vol. 17, Sage Library of Social Research, Sage, New York, 1975.

29 *Ibid.*

30 Gouldner, *op. cit.*, pp. 11–15.

31 Alvin Gouldner, "The Sociologist as Partisan: Sociology and the Welfare State," *American Sociologist*, May 1968, vol. 3, no. 2, pp. 115–16.

32 Carey, *op. cit.*

33 Gouldner, *The Coming Crisis, op.cit.*, p. 493.

34 Jurgen Habermas, *Knowledge and Human Interests*, trans. Jeremy J. Shapiro, Beacon, Boston, 1971, pp. 301–17; and Richard Quinney, *Critique of Legal Order*, Little Brown, Boston, 1974, pp. 11–15.

35 Gabriel Marcel, *The Philosophy of Existentialism*, Citadel, Secaucus, N. J., 1961, p. 128.

36 Martin Heidegger, *Discourse on Thinking*, trans. John M. Anderson and E. Hans Freund, Harper & Row, New York, 1966, p. 53.

37 *Ibid.*

38 Martin Heidegger, *Being and Time*, Harper & Row, New York, 1962, pp. 160ff.

39 Gouldner, *The Coming Crisis, op.cit.*, p. 11.
40 Murray Bookchin, *Post-Scarcity Anarchism*, Ramparts Press, San Francisco, 1971, pp. 210, 179–80.
41 *Ibid.*, p. 17.
42 Berkman, *op.cit.*, p. 233.

1   LAW: AN INSTRUMENT OF AUTHORITY

1   Mikhail Bakunin, *Marxism, Freedom and the State*, trans. and ed. K.J. Kenafick, Freedom, London, 1950, pp. 46–47, as quoted and introduced by Gerald Runkle, *Anarchism Old and New*, Delacorte, New York, 1972, p. 5.
2   R.D. Laing, *The Politics of Experience*, Ballantine, New York, 1967, pp. 11–13.
3   Gabriel Moran, *The Present Revelation: In Quest of Religious Foundations*, Seabury, New York, 1972, p. 82.
4   Milton Mankoff, "Power in Advanced Capitalist Society: A Review Essay on Recent Elitist and Marxist Criticism of Pluralist Theory," *Social Problems*, vol. 17, no. 3, 1970, p. 428; also see Norman Birnbaum, *The Crisis of Industrial Society*, Oxford University Press, New York, 1969; and Ralph Miliband, *The State in Capitalist Society: An Analysis of the Western Systems of Power*, Basic, New York, 1969.
5   April Carter, *The Political Theory of Anarchism*, Harper & Row, New York, 1971, p. 14.
6   Caesare Beccaria, *Essay on Crimes and Punishments*, cited on p. 1, in Ian Taylor, Paul Walton and Jock Young, *The New Criminology*, Routledge & Kegan Paul, London, 1973.
7   Irving Louis Horowitz, ed., *The Anarchists*, Dell, New York, 1964, p. 17.
8   Thomas Merton, *The Asian Journal of Thomas Merton*, New Directions, New York, 1975, p. 332.
9   Alan Watts, *Joyous Cosmology*, Pantheon, New York, 1962, p. 94.
10 Carter, *op.cit.*, p. 22.
11 Clinton Rossiter, *Constitutional Dictatorship: Crisis Government in the Modern Democracies*, Princeton, New Jersey, 1948.
12 Leo Tolstoy, *The Slavery of Our Times*, Dodd Mead, New York, 1900, p. 112.
13 *Ibid.*, p. 123.
14 *Ibid.*, p. 124.
15 Loren Eiseley, *Invisible Pyramid*, Scribner, New York, 1972, p. 144.

16 Runkle, *op. cit.*, p. 75.
17 Tolstoy, *op.cit.*, p. 114.
18 *Ibid.*, p. 105.
19 *Ibid.*, p. 104.
20 Carter, *op.cit.*, p. 114.
21 Lewis Mumford, *The Pentagon of Power*, Harcourt Brace Jovanovich, New York, 1970, p. 284.
22 Carter, *op.cit.*, p. 45.
23 Alvin Gouldner, *The Coming Crisis of Western Sociology*, Basic, New York, 1970, p. 284.
24 Peter Kropotkin, "Law and Authority", *Kropotkin's Revolutionary Pamphlets*, Benjamin Bloom, New York, 1927, pp. 196–218.
25 Mumford, *op.cit.*, p. 283.
26 Albert Parsons, on being sentenced to hang for his beliefs and organizing activities against the merchant princes of Chicago (1886) as quoted in Paul Berman, ed., *Quotations from the Anarchists*, Praeger, New York, 1972, p. 83.
27 Max Stirner as discussed by Daniel Guérin, *Anarchism*, Monthly Review Press, New York, 1970, p. 28.
28 H.L.A. Hart, *Law, Liberty and Morality*, Stanford University Press, 1963; Sanford Kadish, "The Crisis of Over-criminalization," *Annals of the American Academy of Political and Social Sciences*, 347, November 1967; Herbert L. Packer, *The Limits of the Criminal Sanction*, Stanford University Press, 1968.
29 Edwin M. Schur, *Radical Non-Intervention: Rethinking the Delinquency Problem*, Prentice-Hall, Englewood Cliffs, N.J., 1973.
30 Caesare Beccaria, *Essay on Crimes and Punishments*, in Sawyer F. Sylvester, *The Heritage of Modern Criminology*, Schenkman, Cambridge, Mass., 1972, pp. 11–16.
31 Rudolf Rocker, *Anarcho-Syndicalism*, 1930, as quoted in Berman, *op.cit.*, p. 37.
32 Larry L. Tifft, "The Cop Personality: Reconsidered," *Journal of Police Science and Administration*, vol. 2, no. 3, September 1974, pp. 266–78.
33 Peter Kropotkin, "Prisons and Their Moral Influence on Prisoners," *Kropotkin's Revolutionary Pamphlets, op.cit.*; and Alexander Berkman, *Prison Memoirs of An Anarchist*, Mother Earth Publishing Association, New York, 1912.
34 Philip Zimbardo, *et.al.*, "The Psychology of Imprisonment: Privation, Power and Pathology;" The Stanford Prison Experiment, Slide show and unpublished paper, 1971.

35 Larry L. Tifft, Dennis C. Sullivan, and Larry Siegel, "Criminology, Science and Politics," pp. 9–13 in Emilio Viano, ed., *Criminal Justice Research*, Lexington Press, New York, 1975.

36 Paul Goodman, *People or Personnel*, Random House, New York, 1963, p. 184.

37 *Ibid.*, p. 183.

38 Alex Comfort, *Authority and Delinquency in the Modern State: A Criminological Approach to the Problem of Power*, Routledge & Kegan Paul, London, 1950.

39 Benjamin R. Tucker, *Instead of a Book: By A Man Too Busy To Write One*, Tucker, New York, 1897, p. 23.

40 Runkle, *op.cit.*, p. 72.

41 Comfort, *op.cit.*, p. 84.

42 Alexander Berkman, *Now and After: ABC of Communist Anarchism*, Vanguard, New York, 1929, p. 113.

43 Mikhail Bakunin, *Science and the Urgent Revolutionary Task*, 1870, as quoted in Berman, *op. cit.*, pp. 51–52.

44 Eiseley, *op.cit.*, p. 144.

45 *Ibid.*

46 *Ibid.*

47 Henry Adams as quoted in Mumford, *op.cit.*, p. 232.

48 Elisee Reclus, *An Anarchist on Anarchy*, 1886, as quoted in Berman, *op.cit.*, p. 185.

49 Emma Goldman, *The Place of the Individual in Society*, 1930s, as quoted in Berman, *op.cit.*, p. 162.

50 Peter Kropotkin, *Modern Science and Anarchism*, 1913, as quoted in Berman, *op.cit.*, p. 166.

51 Mary Caroline Richards, *Centering in Pottery, Poetry, and the Person*, Wesleyan University Press, Middletown, Conn., 1964, p. 34.

52 Kropotkin, as quoted in Berman, *op.cit.*, p. 166.

53 Emma Goldman, *Anarchism*, 1910, as quoted in Berman, *op.cit.*, p. 163.

54 Runkle, *op.cit.*, p. 55, discussing Proudhon's concept of justice.

55 Pierre Joseph Proudhon, *What Is Property? An Inquiry into the Principle of Right and Government*, trans. Benjamin Tucker, Fertig, New York, 1966, p. 241.

56 Irving Louis Horowitz, ed., *The Anarchists, op.cit.*, p. 204.

57 Berkman, *Now and After, op.cit.*, p. 209.

58 Juan Garcia Oliver, speech in Valencia, 31 Jan. 1937, as quoted in Berman, *op.cit.*, pp. 183–4.

2 SOCIAL HARMS: CRIME AND PENAL SANCTION

1   Mark C. Kennedy, "Beyond Incrimination: Some Neglected Facets of the Theory of Punishment," *Catalyst*, Summer 1970. Quote is from Warner Modular Publication, Reprint 212, p. 3.

2   *Ibid.*, p. 5.

3   *Ibid.*, p. 6.

4   Frederick Engels, *The Origin of the Family, Private Property, and the State*, International Publishers, New York, 1942, p. 97.

5   Richard Quinney, *Critique of Legal Order*, Little, Brown, Boston, 1974, p. 190.

6   *Ibid.*, p. 190.

7   Stanley Diamond, "The Rule of Law Versus the Order of Custom," in Robert Paul Wolff, ed., *The Rule of Law*, Simon and Schuster, New York, 1971, p. 140.

8   Kennedy, *op.cit.*, p. 7.

9   *Ibid.*, p. 10. Kennedy draws on Marc Bloch, *Feudal Society*, trans. L.A. Manyon, University of Chicago Press, 1964.

10 Bloch, *op.cit.*, pp. 123–5.

11 Kennedy, *op.cit.*, p. 16. See also Egon Bittner and Anthony Platt, "The Meaning of Punishment," 2, *Issues in Criminology*, 82, 1966.

12 *Ibid.* See also George Rusche and Otto Kirchheimer, *Punishment and Social Structure*, Columbia University Press, New York, 1939, ch. 2.

13 Alexander Berkman, *Now and After: ABC of Communist Anarchism*, Vanguard, New York, 1929, p. 69.

14 David M. Gordon, "Capitalism, Class and Crime in America," *Crime and Delinquency*, April 1973, p. 179.

15 *Ibid.* See Paul Sweezy, "The State," ch. 13, *The Theory of Capitalist Development*, Monthly Review Press, New York, 1968.

16 *Ibid.*, p. 179, see his footnote 52.

17 Kennedy, *op.cit.*, p. 19.

18 John Lofland, *Deviance and Identity*, Prentice.Hall, Englewood Cliffs, N.J., 1969, p. 287.

19 C.Wright Mills, "The Professional Ideology of Social Pathologists," *American Journal of Sociology*, 49, Sept. 1943, pp. 165–80.

20 Lofland, *op.cit.*, p. 287.

21 *Ibid.*

22 Peter Marris and Martin Rein, *The Dilemmas of Social Reform: Poverty and Community Action In the United States*, Atherton, New York, 1967.

23 Joseph Helfgot, "Professional Reform Organizations and the Symbolic Representation of the Poor," *American Sociological Review*, vol. 34, no. 4, August 1974, pp. 475–91.

24 Daniel Patrick Moynihan, *Maximum Feasible Misunderstanding: Community Action in the War on Poverty*, Free Press, New York, 1969.

25 William Ryan, *Blaming the Victim*, Random House, New York, 1971.

26 Lewis A. Coser, "Some Functions of Deviant Behaviour and Normative Flexability," *American Journal of Sociology*, vol. 68., Sept. 1962, pp. 172–81, esp. p. 174.

27 Lofland, *op.cit.*, pp. 302–3.

28 Robert A. Dentler and Kai T. Erikson, "The Functions of Deviance in Groups," *Social Problems*, vol. 7, 1959, pp. 98–107.

29 Joseph R. Gusfield, "Moral Passage: The Symbolic Process in the Public Designation of Deviance," *Social Problems*, vol. 15, fall 1967, pp. 175–88.

30 Talcott Parsons, "Deviant Behaviour and Social Control," ch. 7 in *The Social System*, Free Press, New York, 1951, p. 309.

31 *Ibid.*, p. 309.

32 *Ibid.*, p. 308.

33 *Ibid.*, p. 309.

34 *Ibid.*, p. 265.

35 Quinney, *op.cit.*, p. 86. For a good illustration of this see the centralistic proposals in Committee for Economic Development. *Reducing Crime and Assuring Justice*, Committee for Economic Development, New York, 1972.

36 See *Night and Fog*, Alain Resnais' brilliant and powerful cinema documentary on the concepts of authority and hierarchy in the Nazi concentration camps, 1955.

37 Barry Krisberg, *Crime and Privilege*, Prentice-Hall, Englewood Cliffs, N.J., 1975, p. 136.

38 *Ibid.*, p. 140. This section, like Krisberg's, is based heavily on George Rusche and Otto Kirchheimer, *Punishment and Social Structure*, Russell and Russell, New York, 1968.

39 *Ibid.*, p. 144.

40 *Ibid.*, p. 148.

41 Peter Kropotkin, *In Russian and French Prisons*, Schocken, New

York, 1971. Exile and "freeman" prisoners were transported to Siberia. From the mid 1700s to the late 1800s, 1,200,000 exiles were transported by foot and train to Siberia. Many of the exploitative control tactics described were those of the robber/merchant barons of American capitalism such as Carnegie-Frick and Pullman.

42 David J. Rothman, "The Changing Role of the Asylum," *Public Interest*, vol. 26, 1972, pp. 3–17.

43 Alvin Gouldner, *The Coming Crisis of Western Sociology*, Basic Books, New York, 1971, pp. 62–3.

44 Ian Taylor, Paul Walton, Jock Young, *The New Criminology: for a Social Theory of Deviance*, Routledge & Kegan Paul, London, 1973, p. 2.

45 David Matza, *Becoming Deviant*, Prentice-Hall, Englewood Cliffs, N.J., 1969, p. 197.

46 Taylor, Walton, Young, *op.cit.*, p. 2.

47 *Ibid.*; Taylor, Walton, Young are excerpting from Caesare Beccaria, *Essay on Crimes and Punishment*, 1st American edition Stephen Gould, New York, 1809, p. 12.

48 *Ibid.*, p. 2. Also see p. 21 and Beccaria *op.cit.*, pp. 23–4.

49 *Ibid.*, p. 2.

50 *Ibid.*, pp. 20–1, and Beccaria *op.cit.*, pp. 11, 13–17.

51 Taylor, Walton, Young, *op.cit.*, p. 22.

52 *Ibid.*, p. 2.; Beccaria, *op.cit.*, p. 11.

53 *Ibid.*, p. 3.

54 David Fogel, *We Are The Living Proof: The Justice Model for Corrections*, W.H. Anderson, Cincinnati, Ohio, 1975, p. 19.

55 David Rothman, *The Discovery of the Asylum*, Little Brown, Boston, 1971, pp. 485–6, as quoted in Fogel, *Ibid.*, pp. 19–29.

56 Norman B. Johnston, "John Haviland," in *Pioneers in Criminology*, ed. Herman Mannheim, Stevens, London, 1960, p. 108.

57 Chester W. Wright, *Economic History of The United States*, McGraw-Hill, New York, 1941, p. 236.

58 David Rothman, "The Invention of the Penitentiary," *Criminal Law Bulletin*, vol. 8, no. 7, 1972, p. 558.

59 Paul Takagi, "The Walnut Street Jail: A Penal Reform to Centralize the Powers of the State," *Federal Probation*, Dec. 1975, vol. 39, no. 4, pp. 18–25.

60 *Ibid.*, p. 24.

61 Alexander Liazos, "Class Oppression: The Functions of Juve-

nile Justice," *The Insurgent Sociologist*, VI, fall 1974, pp. 2–24.

62   Martin B. Miller, "At Hard Labor: Rediscovery of the 19th Century Prison," *Issues in Criminology*, vol. 9, no. 1, spring, 1974, pp. 91–111.

63   Paul Takagi, "The Correctional System," *Crime and Social Justice*, 2, fall-winter 1974, p. 82.

64   *Ibid.*, p. 84.

65   Alexander Berkman, *Prison Memoirs of an Anarchist*, Schocken, New York, 1970.

66   Matza, *op.cit.*

67   For further elaboration of these comparisons see: William J. Chambliss, "Functional and Conflict Theories of Crime," *MSS Modular Publication*, Module 17, 1973, pp. 1–23; John Horton, "Order and Conflict Theories of Social Problems As Competing Ideologies," *American Journal of Sociology*, vol. 71. May 1966, pp. 701–13; John Griffiths, "Ideology in Criminal Procedure or a Third 'Model' of the Criminal Process," *Yale Law Journal*, vol. 79, no. 3, 1970, pp. 359–417.

68   Taylor, Walton, Young, *op.cit.*, Ch. 1–2.

69   Leon Radzinowicz, *Ideology and Crime: A Study of Crime in its Social and Historical Context*, Heinemann, London, 1966.

70   Krisberg, *op.cit.*, p. 165.

71   Alvin W. Gouldner, "The Sociologist as Partisan: Sociology and the Welfare State," *The American Sociologist*, May 1968, pp. 103–16.

72   John Horton, "The Dehumanization of Anomie and Aliena- tion: A Problem in the Ideology of Sociology," *British Journal of Sociology*, 1964, pp. 283–300.

73   See Taylor, Walton, Young, *op.cit.*, p. 86; Emile Durkheim, *The Division of Labor in Society*, Free Press, New York, 1964.

74   See Edwin M. Schur, *Radical Non-Intervention: Rethinking the Delinquency Problem*, Prentice-Hall, Englewood Cliffs, N.J., 1973; also see David Matza, *Delinquency and Drift*, Wiley, New York, 1964, and David Matza, *Becoming Deviant*, Prentice- Hall, Englewood Cliffs, N.J., 1969.

75   Gouldner, "The Sociologist as Partisan," *op.cit.*, p. 106.

76   *Ibid.*, p. 107.

77   Taylor, Walton, Young, *op.cit.*, p. 30.

78   Matza, *Becoming Deviant, op.cit.*, pp. 92–93.

79   Lloyd E. Ohlin, *Prisoners In America*, Prentice-Hall, Englewood Cliffs, N.J., 1973.

80   Gouldner, *op. cit.*, p. 107.
81   Patrick McAnany, "Jerome Miller In Illinois: Due Process As An Obstacle To Change," unpublished paper, 1975; Also see Barbara Stolz, "The Massachusetts Department of Youth Services 1969–1973; A Study of How Policy Change Within An Agency is Accepted by its External Political Environment," Ph. D. dissertation, Brandeis, 1975; John M. Martin and Gerald M. Shattuk, "Community Interaction and the Correctional Mandate," unpublished paper, 1967.
82   Barton L. Ingraham and Gerald W. Smith, "The Use of Electronics in the Observation and Control of Human Behavior and Its Possible Use in Rehabilitation and Parole," *Issues in Criminology*, vol. 7, no. 2, 1972, p. 35.
83   *Ibid.*, p. 50.
84   Michael H. Shapiro, "The Uses of Behavior Control Technologies: A Response," *Issues in Criminology*, vol. 7, no. 2, 1972, pp. 55–99.
85   Ralph K. Schwitzgebel, "Limitations on the Coercive Treatment of Offenders," *Criminal Law Bulletin*, vol. 8, no. 4, pp. 267–320. Also see Ralph K. Schwitzgebel, *Development and Legal Regulation of Coercive Behaviour Modification Techniques With Offenders*, National Institute of Mental Health, 1971.
86   Jessica Mitford, *Kind and Usual Punishment*, Random House, New York, 1971; Erik Olin Wright, *The Politics of Punishment*, Harper, New York, 1973.
87   Fogel, *op.cit.*
88   James Q. Wilson, *Thinking About Crime*, New York, Basic Books, 1975; Gary S. Becker, "Crime and Punishment: An Economic Approach," *Journal of Political Economy*, March–April, 1968; Ernest van den Haag, *Punishing Criminals: Concerning A Very Old and Painful Question*, Basic Books, New York, 1975.
89   Nicholas N. Kittrie, *The Right To Be Different*, Penguin, Baltimore, 1973, p. 298.
90   Patrick D. McAnany, book review of Kittrie's *The Right to be Different* in *Journal of Criminal Law, Criminology and Police Science*, vol. 63, no. 4, pp. 557–60. Kittrie believes that the therapeutic state has evolved historically through humanitarian motivation. Though this motivation may have been involved it certainly was accompanied by control motives and policies of recognized safety valve effect. See Robert A. Burt, *op.cit.*

189

91 James O'Connor, *The Fiscal Crisis of the State*, St Martins Press, New York, 1973.

92 H.C. Greisman and Kurt Finsterbush, "The Unprofitability of Warfare: An Historical–Quantitative Approach," *Social Problems*, vol. 22, no. 3, Feb. 1975, pp. 450–63.

93 *Ibid.*; Gregory McLauchlan, "LEAA: A Case Study in the Development of the Social Industrial Complex," *Crime and Social Justice*, 4, 1975, pp. 15–23.

94 David Horowitz, *Empire and Revolution: A Radical Interpretation of Contemporary History*, Random House, New York, 1969, pp. 257–8, as quoted in Quinney, *Critique of Legal Order, op.cit.*, p. 94.

95 Huey Newton in Kai Erikson, ed., *In Search of Common Ground: Conversations with Huey Newton and Erik Erikson*, W.W. Norton, New York, 1974.

96 Peter Arshinov, *History of the Makhnovist Movement (1918–1921)*, Black & Red, Detroit, and Solidarity, Chicago, 1974, p. 153.

97 Paul Takagi, "A Garrison State in a 'Democratic' Society," *Crime and Social Justice*, 1, spring–summer 1974, pp. 27–33.

98 Alex Comfort, *Authority and Delinquency in the Modern State*, Routledge & Kegan Paul, London, 1950, p. IX.

99 Herman and Julia Schwendinger, "Defenders of Order or Guardians of Human Rights," *Issues in Criminology*, vol. 5, no. 2, summer, 1970, pp. 123–57; Anthony Platt, "Prospects for a Radical Criminology in the United States," *Crime and Social Justice*, 1, spring–summer, 1974, pp. 2–10; Also see Quinney, *Critique of Legal Order, op. cit.*

100 Peter Kropotkin, *Mutual Aid*, Extending Horizons Books, Porter Sargent, 1914 original; Peter Kropotkin, *Ethics: Origin and Development*, Dial, New York, 1924.

101 Joseph W. Rodgers and M.D. Buffalo, "Fighting Back: Nine Modes of Adaptation to a Deviant Label," *Social Problems*, vol. 22, no. 1, 1974, pp. 101–18.

102 Susan Gilmore and Dean Selock, "Rape Rebuttal," *Black Star*, vol. 1, no. 2, pp. 4–6, quote from p. 6.

103 John Lennon and Yoko Ono, "Woman is the Nigger of the World," Copyright 1972, Ono Music, Inc.; also claimed by Maclean Music, Inc. Northern Songs/BMI.

104 Social Revolutionary Anarchist Federation, "The Anarchist Solution to The Problem of Crime," A SRAF New Directions Series Pamphlet, Chicago, no date, p. 6.

105   Elliott Currie, book review: "Beyond Criminology," a review
      of *The New Criminology*, in *Issues in Criminology*, vol. 9, no. 1,
      spring, 1974, pp. 133–46. Currie, in an excellent review, feels
      that the book, "promotes an image of the deviant as a roman-
      tic, if inarticulate, rebel against the conventions of an oppress-
      ive society." He asks, "Does the criminality of the Nixon
      administration (the powerful) represent 'inarticulate striving'
      against the conditions of oppression?" Well, no, of course not,
      they are not the oppressed. But it does represent an expression
      of an oppressive political order, an extension of that order.
      After all, their criminality was in the context of oppress/
      compete/dominate, or be dominated. It is plausible that the
      Nixon administration's (harms) acts occurred in the context
      of other elites attempting to incapacitate Nixon and those
      interests he represented. In the same context, we do not see
      rape as a politically progressive act. Certainly it is a response
      to sexism, authority, invasion and control. Is it possible to
      determine what is and what is not politically progressive? *No
      political acts (acts to control others) are progressive!* Is there a real
      difference between modes of control or social harm? Does it
      matter if one progressively or retrogressively controls another
      person?
106   Michael Bakunin, "Social and Economic Bases of Anar-
      chism," in Irving Louis Horowitz, ed., *The Anarchists, op. cit.*,
      p. 136.
107   Richard Quinney, "From Repression to Liberation: Social
      Theory In a Radical Age, ch. 12, p. 335, in Robert A. Scott
      and Jack D. Douglas, eds., *Theoretical Perspectives on Deviance*,
      New York, Basic, pp, 317–41.

3   THE STATE

1   Reinhard Bendix, "Bureaucracy: The Problem And Its Set-
    ting," *American Sociological Review*, 12, Oct. 1947, p. 495.
2   H.H. Gerth and C. Wright Mills, *From Max Weber: Essays in
    Sociology*, Oxford, New York, 1946, pp. 196–224.
3   Ernest Barker, *The Development of Public Services in Western Europe
    1660–1930*, Oxford, New York, 1944, p. 6.
4   Reinhard Bendix, "The Impact of Ideas on Organizational
    Structure", *Work and Authority in Industry*, Wiley, New York,
    1956, pp. 1–21.
5   *Ibid.*

6   *Ibid.*

7   *Ibid.*

8   *Ibid.*

9   Peter Arshinov, *History of the Makhnovist Movement (1918–1921)*, Black and Red, Detroit, and Solidarity, Chicago, 1974, p. 67.

10 *Ibid.*, p. 85.

11 Rudolf Rocker, "Anarchism and Anarcho-Syndicalism," pp. 225–68 in Paul Eltzbacher, ed., *Anarchism*, Freedom, London, 1960. Rocker is quoting Kropotkin.

12 Rudolf Rocker, *op. cit.*

13 Gil Green, *The New Radicalism: Anarchist or Marxist?*, International, New York, 1971, p. 26.

14 *Ibid.*

15 Karl Shapiro, "On the Revival of Anarchism," *Liberation*, February, 1961.

16 Daniel Guerin, *Anarchism: From Theory to Practice*, Monthly Review Press, New York, 1970, p. 16.

17 Noam Chomsky, *American Power and the New Mandarins*, Pantheon, New York, 1969, p. 317.

18 *Ibid.*, p. 72.

19 *Ibid.*, p. 135; Cited in Paul Avrich, *The Russian Anarchists*, Princeton University Press, 1967, pp. 93–4.

20 *Ibid.*, p. 135; Anton Pannekoek, *Workers Councils*, Melbourne, 1950, pp. 36–7.

21 *Ibid.*, p. 317–8.

22 *Ibid.*, p. 345.

23 *Ibid.*, p. 345; see pp. 323–47, for the full argument and critique of Daniel Bell's essay on the end of ideology in the West, in welfare states. Also see Daniel Bell, *The End of Ideology*, Free Press, New York, 1960, pp. 335–68.

24 *Ibid.*, p. 402.

25 *Ibid.*, p. 27.

26 *Ibid.*, p. 125.

27 *Ibid.*, p. 319.

28 *Ibid.*

29 *Ibid.*

30 Jonathan Kozol as quoted in Sheldon Frank, "The Education of Jonathan Kozol," a review of Kozol's book, *The Night Is Dark and I am Far From Home, Reader, Chicago's Free Weekly*, Friday, 16 January 1976, v. 5, no. 15.

31 Chloë Schreiner, "The State as 'protector'," p. 7, *The Match*,

Nov. 1974.

32 *Ibid.*

33 Mikhail Bakunin, *The Political Philosophy of Bakunin*, G. P. Maximoff, ed., Free Press, 1964, p. 138.

34 Peter Kropotkin, *Words of a Rebel, 1885*, as quoted in Paul Berman, *Quotations from the Anarchists*, Praeger, New York, 1972, p. 48.

35 Bakunin, *The Political Philosophy, op. cit.*, pp. 77–81.

36 Richard Quinney, *Critique of Legal Order*, Little, Brown, Boston, 1974, p. 132.

37 Paul Takagi, "The Walnut Street Jail: A Penal Reform to Centralize the Powers of the State," *Federal Probation*, Dec. 1975, vol. 39, no. 4, pp. 18–26.

38 James Weinstein, *The Corporate Ideal in the Liberal State: 1900–1918*, Beacon, Boston, 1969.

39 Milton Mankoff, "Power in Advanced Capitalist Society: A Review Essay On Recent Elitist and Marxist Criticism of Pluralist Theory," *Social Problems*, vol. 17, no. 3, 1970, pp. 418–30; William Domhoff, *Who Rules America?*, Prentice-Hall, Englewood Cliffs, N. J., 1967, pp. 63–77; William Domhoff, "Where a Pluralist Goes Wrong?," *Berkeley Journal of Sociology*, vol. 14, 1968, pp. 39–48.

40 Gil Green, *The New Radicalism: Anarchist or Marxist?*, International, New York, 1971, p. 46.

41 Ralph Miliband, *The State In Capitalist Society*, Basic, New York, 1969, p. 272.

42 Bertram Gross, "Friendly Fascism, A Model for America," *Social Policy*, 1, 1970, p. 46.

43 *Ibid.*, p. 48.

44 Willard Waller, "Social Problems and the Mores," *American Sociological Review*, Dec. 1936, pp. 924–30.

45 Willard Waller asserts that: "Probably the humanitarian impulse has always existed, but it has apparently attained group-wide expression at a relatively late period in our history, following the breakdown of primary group society. Social problems in the modern sense did not exist when every primary group cared for its own helpless and unfortunate. Social problems as we know them are a phenomenon of secondary group society, in which the primary group is no longer willing and able to take care of its members. It was this breakdown which called group-wide humanitarianism into existence; it was this

situation which brought it about that we were asked to feel sympathy for those whom we had never seen. Humanitarian mores are frequently expressed, for they are highly verbal, and they command the instant assent of almost any group."

46 *Ibid.*
47 *Ibid.*
48 *Ibid.*
49 *Ibid.*
50 Barrington Moore, Jr, *Reflections on the Causes of Human Misery: And Upon Certain Proposals to Eliminate Them*, Beacon Press, Boston, 1972, pp. 1–2.
51 *Ibid.*, Chapter 2.
52 See footnote 10; the peasants of the region when no longer constrained, managed, by external political authority created free workers' communes and councils (1918–1919). Chomsky in his essay on "Objectivity and Liberal Scholarship" (*American Power and the New Mandarins, op. cit.* p. 123) cites a study of collectivization published by the CNT in 1937 which concludes with a description of the village of Membrilla. "In its miserable huts live the poor inhabitants of a poor province; eight thousand people, but the streets are not paved, the town has no newspaper, no cinema, neither a cafe nor a library. On the other hand, it has many churches that have been burned." Immediately after the Franco insurrection, the land was expropriated and village life collectivized. "Food, clothing, and tools were distributed equitably to the whole population. Money was abolished, work collectivized, all goods passed to the community, consumption was socialized. It was, however, not a socialization of wealth but of poverty. Work continued as before. An elected council appointed committees to organize the life of the commune and its relations to the outside world. The necessities of life were distributed freely, insofar as they were available. A large number of refugees were accommodated. A small library was established, and a small school of design."

The document closes with these words: "The whole population lived as in a large family; functionaries, delegates, the secretary of the syndicates, the members of the municipal council, all elected, acted as heads of a family. But they were controlled, because special privilege or corruption would not be tolerated. Membrilla is perhaps the poorest village of Spain, but it is the most just."

53   Murray Bookchin, *Post-Scarcity Anarchism*, Ramparts Press, San Francisco, 1971.

54   Moore, *op. cit.*, ch. 3.

55   Chomsky, *op. cit., American Power and the New Mandarins*, p. 18.

56   Colin Ward, *Anarchy in Action*, Harper, New York, 1974.

57   Gustave Landauer, "Weak Statesmen, Weaker People," *Der Sozialist*, June 1910.

58   Mikhail Bakunin as cited by Noam Chomsky in his introduction to Daniel Guerin, *Anarchism*, Monthly Review Press, New York, 1970, p. x.

59   Chomsky, *Ibid.*, p. xi.

60   John Rawls, *A Theory of Justice*, Harvard University Press, Cambridge, Mass., 1971.

61   James S. Coleman, "Review Essay: Inequality, Sociology, and Moral Philosophy," *American Journal of Sociology*, vol. 80, 1974, no. 3, pp. 745–6. Rawls's two principles of the just order are: (1) Each person is to have an equal right to the most extensive basic liberty compatible with a similar liberty for others; (2) Social and economic inequalities are to be arranged so that they are both (a) reasonably expected to be to everyone's advantage, and (b) attached to positions and offices open to all. Coleman feels that the second principle justifies inequalities which make everyone better off, especially the least advantaged. In this sense he describes Rawls's formulation as a greater constraint than the efficiency criterion of utilitarianism which justifies inequalities on a productivity (not distributive) base.

62   Noam Chomsky, *For Reasons of State*, Pantheon, New York, 1973, page after title page – quote is from Bakunin.

63   Noam Chomsky, *Problems of Knowledge and Freedom: The Russell Lectures*, "On Changing the World", reference to Russell's view of Socialism, p. 60, Pantheon, N.Y., 1971.

64   Colin Ward, *Anarchy in Action, op. cit.*, p. 11.

65   Leo Tolstoy, "Appeal to Social Reformers", pp. 100–17 in Waldo R. Browne, *Man or the State*, Huebsch, New York, 1919.

66   *Ibid.*, p. 108.

67   Barrington Moore, *op. cit.*, ch. 3, pp. 74–5. Moore's four questions are as follows: "(1) How can the type of rivalries that have so far always plagued independent political units be avoided under the situation of a series of anarchist communities?; (2) What may happen due to the fact that some anar-

chist communities will be much wealthier than others and have control of resources that others require?; (3) Presumably such difficulties would be less severe in a less materialistic and partly de-industrialized world. But just how much de-industrialization and of what kind would a neo-anarchist advocate in the light of the world's population and economic interdependence?; (4) Would neo-anarchist societies be able to control innate tendencies towards the growth of the trader, the manipulator, the fixer, without creating such a restrictive moral code and enforcing it by such nosy and inquisitorial methods as to cast a repressive miasma over the whole culture?" Moore feels that self management is a device to oppose the abuses of authority not a possible substitute for central authority or a resolution to the problem of how to control authority. (p. 68)

68 *Ibid.*, p. 135.

69 We would attribute this negative prospectus to Moore's historically incomplete or misleading presentation of attempts at direct democracy, anarchist notions of democracy, and his logically unsupported assumptions regarding the necessity of central authority.

"Direct democracy brings to mind the theory and practice behind such experiments in popular control as the meetings of the Paris sections of the sans-culottes during the brief period well prior to Robespierre's fall when they had some real power, and also the Russian soviets during a period that was also very brief when they exercised some real power. A key point in all these arrangements is that they did provide an opportunity, even if by no means a full one, for the victims of the social order to make their own voices heard. At this point in time revolutionary terror had temporarily removed from the arena that portion of the political spectrum that in 'normal' times is the most articulate, namely of course the old elites. But in a very short space of time revolutionary terror turned against direct democracy. The usual explanation is the necessity for the restoration of order, the impossibility of taking into account by such means the general requirements of the whole society, of reaching and coordinating decisions through myriad separate groups of uneducated people. That is indeed a crucial part of the story. But it leaves out of account whose law and order was restored and to whose benefit the restoration took place. In general, it is safe to assert that the restoration of order and security has not been for the benefit of the little people in whose honor the revolutions were proclaimed. Nor is it possible, I think, to separate the original use of the revolutionary terror against the old elite from its later use against the little people. Direct democracy generates revolutionary terror, its own nemesis." (pp. 65–6).

There are several points to be made about this argument: (1) Are the old elites the most articulate in the political spectrum? (2) The law and order restored was not that of the social revolutionaries, little people. (3) Moore does not discuss Spain, a clearer example of the potentialities of anarchism. (4) Does Moore stake a claim against revolutionary terror as a means of revolution? If so, we agree. (5) *It does not follow from Moore's argument that direct democracy generates revolutionary terror.* Revolutionary terror was generated by the new elites, authoritarian usurpers and users of the revolutionary condition. This terror was imposed on the people from without, supported in Russia by Western ruling elites, not generated by direct democracy. Moore's argument in this section and in assessment of anarchism assumes the necessity for elites, authority (p. 76). Numerous historical accounts demonstrate Moore's incomplete presentation of historical fact (Voline, Chomsky, Kropotkin, Guerin, etc.) in this argument. Moore himself presents a more full account in a latter section of the book (p. 177). His assumption of the necessity of authoritarian centralization is least supported and most disturbing.

70 George Bernard Shaw, "The Impossibilities of Anarchism", in Leonard Krimerman and Lewis Perry, *Patterns of Anarchy*, Anchor Books, New York, 1966, p. 509.

71 Bertrand Russell, "Proposed Roads to Freedom: Socialism, Anarchism, and Syndicalism," in Krimerman and Perry, *op. cit.*, pp. 491–2. The following is Russell's argument: "The conclusion, which appears to be forced upon us, is that the anarchist ideal of a community in which no acts are forbidden by law is not, at any rate for the present, compatible with the stability of such a world as the anarchists desire. In order to obtain and preserve a world resembling as closely as possible that at which they aim, it will still be necessary that some acts should be forbidden by law. We may put the chief of these under three heads: (1) Theft (2) Crimes of Violence (3) The creation of organizations intended to subvert the Anarchist regime by

force . . .

"1. Theft. It is true that in an Anarchist world there will be no destitution, and therefore no thefts motivated by starvation. But such thefts are at present by no means the most considerable or the most harmful. The system of rationing which is to be applied to luxuries, will leave many men with fewer luxuries than they might desire. It will give opportunities for speculation by those who are in control of the public stores, and it will leave the possibility of appropriating such valuable objects of art as would naturally be preserved in public museums. It may be contended that such forms of theft would be prevented by public opinion. But public opinion is not greatly operative upon an individual unless it is the opinion of his own group. A group of men combined for purposes of theft might readily defy the public opinion of the majority unless that public opinion made itself effective by the use of force against them. Probably, in fact, such force would be applied through popular indignation, but in that case we should revive the evils of the criminal law with the added evils of uncertainty, haste and passion, which are inseparable from the practice of lynching. If, as we have suggested, it were found necessary to provide an economic stimulus to work by allowing fewer luxuries to idlers, this would afford a new motive for theft on their part and a new necessity for some form of criminal law.

"2. Crimes of Violence. Cruelty to children, crimes of jealousy, rape and so forth, are almost certain to occur in any society to some extent. The prevention of such acts is essential to the existence of freedom for the weak. If nothing were done to hinder them, it is to be feared that the customs of a society would gradually become rougher, and that acts which are now rare would cease to be so. If Anarchists are right in maintaining that the existence of such an economic system as they desire would prevent the commission of crimes of this kind, the laws forbidding them would do no harm to liberty. If, on the other hand, the impulse to such actions persisted, it would be necessary that steps should be taken to restrain men from indulging it.

"3. The third class of difficulties is much the most serious and involves much the most drastic interference with liberty. I don't see how a private army could be tolerated within an Anarchist community, and I do not see how it could be prevented except by a general prohibition of carrying arms. If there were no such prohibition, rival parties would organize rival forces, and civil war would result. Yet, if there is such a prohibition, it cannot well be carried out without a very considerable interference with individual liberty. No doubt, after a time, the idea of using violence to achieve a political object might die down, as the practice of duelling has done. But such changes of habit and outlook are facilitated by legal prohibition and would hardly come about without it. At present a very large part of the criminal law is concerned in safeguarding the rights of property, that is to say – as things are now – the unjust privileges of the rich. Those whose principles lead them into conflict with government, like Anarchists, bring a most formidable indictment against the law and the authorities for the unjust manner in which they support the status quo. Many of the actions by which men have become rich are far more harmful to the community than the obscure crimes of poor men, yet they go unpunished because they do not interfere with the existing order. If the power of the community is to be brought to bear to prevent certain classes of actions through the agency of the criminal law, it is as necessary that these actions should really be those which are harmful to the community, as it is that the treatment of "criminals" should be freed from the conception of guilt and inspired by the same spirit as is shown in the treatment of disease. But, if these two conditions were fulfilled, I cannot help thinking that a society which preserved the existence of law would be preferable to one conducted on the unadulterated principles of Anarchism.

"We may now sum up our discussion of the powers of Government.

"The State, in spite of what Anarchists urge, seems a necessary institution for certain purposes. Peace and war, tariffs, regulation of sanitary conditions and of the sale of noxious drugs, the preservation of a just system of distribution: these, among others, are functions which could hardly be performed in a community in which there was no central government. Take, for example, the liquor traffic, or the opium traffic in China. If alcohol could be obtained at cost price without taxation, still more of it could be obtained for nothing, as Anarchists presumably desire; can we believe that there would not be a great and disastrous increase of drunkenness? China was brought to the verge of ruin by opium, and every patriotic Chinaman desired to see the traffic in opium restricted. In such matters freedom is not a panacea, and some degree of legal restriction seems imperative for the national health."

72   *Ibid.* p. 492.
73   D.H. Monro, "Godwin's Moral Philosophy", in Krimerman and Perry, *op. cit.*, p. 545.
74   Gabriel Kolko, *The Roots of American Foreign Policy*, Beacon, Boston, 1969.
75   Harry Magdoff, *The Age of Imperialism: The Economics of U.S. Foreign Policy*, Monthly Review Press, New York, 1969.
76   Paul A. Baran, *The Political Economy of Growth*, Monthly Review Press, New York, 1957; Paul A. Baran and Paul M. Sweezy, *Monopoly Capital*, Monthly Review Press, New York, 1966.
77   Herbert Marcuse, *One-Dimensional Man*, Beacon, Boston, 1964.
78   Moore addresses this point in an illuminating discussion as the absence of a demand for change. It is important to note the word *demand*, as this implies authority relations such that someone has the power to meet these demands – that the miseries could be minimized by political authorities toward whom the demands would be directed. Our use of the phrase consciousness of a need for change implies that individuals cannot rely on political/authority structures but rather must themselves change. Nevertheless Moore's comments regarding American society are interesting. (pp. 144–6 in Moore, *op. cit.*)

"Though the forces that push American society in the direction of domination and oppression are indeed powerful, they do not constitute some sort of insuperable imperative built into the very structure of its social order. The predatory solution to its domestic social problems is neither a necessary solution, nor the only solution. Rather it is merely the most obvious one, and in the short run the pleasantest, easiest, and cheapest for a very large number of American citizens.

"Nor are the main reasons very difficult to discern. For a very large part of the population the chief costs of the predatory solution fall upon outsiders, mainly now people with dark skins in Asia and Latin America. Such persons are therefore outside the tenuous bonds of indentification felt with those who share in Western 'advanced' culture. To a lesser and much more indirect extent the costs also fall upon outsiders in American society itself, notably the bottom layers of the population, a large proportion of which also has dark skins, and whose needs are neglected in favor of the investment in destruction. Even many of these, however, make some gains from the predatory solution that are likely to be immediate and tangible, such as temporary escape from the ghetto into the armed forces, while neglect remains merely pervasive. Still others share in the gain, even if far from equally. For workers, jobs are preferable to anything that smacks of a dole.

"Why should huge segments of the public demand change, as long as others bear the main costs of predatory policies and the mass of the population makes some minor gains from them? Or, one could say, as long as their losses take the form of slow deterioration in the urban environment, increasing inconvenience, or doing without the advantages of civilization that the masses never learned to want very badly – hospitals, schools, housing, clean air. These are issues about which it is impossible to arouse political passions, though they are matters about which Americans will make enormous individual efforts, once past a certain level of economic achievement. The main preoccupation of most people is likely to remain as usual, with private concerns. Their attitude towards politics, I would suggest, is one of mildly grumbling indifference, with not so latent aggressive tendencies towards any individual or group that threatens daily routines or the limited security of their sources of livelihood. Perhaps many of them would go along very happily and willingly with a better society, one that made a more humane use of its resources and a less destructive one, if it became for them as individuals a real and immediate possibility. But they are not likely to do anything about it on their own, or as a collective undertaking. Furthermore, a whole host of experiences and traditions based on these experiences, where they have had to pay the freight for well-meant efforts at improvement, makes very many Americans resistant to and suspicious of "outsiders" who attempt to organize them for any colllective undertaking that smacks of overturning the social world to which they have become accustomed."

79 Tolstoy, *op. cit.*, p. 109.
80 *Ibid.*, p. 113.
81 Bertrand Russell, agreeing with Tolstoy, felt that "the real obstacles lie in the heart of man, and the cure for these is a firm hope, informed and fortified by thought"; quoted from

201

Chomsky, *Problems of Knowledge and Freedom, op. cit.*, p. 62.

82 Oscar Wilde, "The Soul of Man under Socialism", in Waldo R. Browne, *Man or the State*, Huebsch, New York, 1919, pp. 131–2.

83 *Ibid.*, p. 135.

84 Pat Jordan, "Hard Times – New Vision", *The Catholic Worker*, vol. 40 no. 8, Oct.–Nov. 1974. The critical issue is environmental destruction and thus we generally advocate decentralized energy. Tidal power is necessarily capital intensive and solar power is ineffective in high latitudes, thus possibly requiring capital intensive solar generation at low latitudes. But again, we wish to stress non-destructive energy production and decentralization.

85 *Ibid.*

86 Ernest Friedrick Schumacher, *Small is Beautiful: A Study of Economics as if People Mattered*, Harper & Row, New York, 1973.

87 See Daniel Guérin, *Anarchism: From Theory to Practice*, Monthly Review Press, New York, 1970, for an excellent review.

88 Robert Ellisberg, "Self-rule," *The Catholic Worker*, vol. 41, no. 9, Dec. 1975.

4 THE WISH TO BE FREE: COMMITMENT TO EDEN

1 Gabriel Moran, *Present Revelation: In Quest of Religious Foundations*, Herder and Herder, New York, 1972, p. 119.

2 Murray Bookchin, *Post-Scarcity Anarchism*, Ramparts Press, San Francisco, 1971, p. 22.

3 Moran, *op. cit.*, pp. 125–6.

4 John Dewey, *Art as Experience*, Putnam, New York, 1958, p. 122.

5 Fred Weinstein and Gerald M. Platt, *The Wish To Be Free*, University of California Press, Berkeley, California, 1973, p. 219.

6 *Ibid.*, pp 210–20.

7 *Ibid.*, p. 220.

8 *Ibid.*, p. 221.

9 *Ibid.*

10 Christopher Lash, "The Emotions of Family Life," *The New York Review of Books*, 27 November 1975, pp. 37–42.

11 Moran, *op. cit.*, p. 72.

12 Lash, *op. cit.*, p. 42

13 *Ibid.*, p. 39.

14 *Ibid.*, p. 40.

15 *Ibid.*

16   Noam Chomsky, "Objectivity and Liberal Scholarship," in *American Power and the New Mandarins*, Pantheon, New York, 1969.

17   Weinstein and Platt, *op. cit.*, pp. 224–5.

18   *Ibid.*, p. 225.

19   Perhaps some processes seem to end, but there are no resolutions for the dialectics of social life. More specifically, we are talking about revolution as a never-ending process. "The revolution is in the individual spirit, or it is nowhere. If it is seen as having an end, it will never truly begin." – Ursula Le Guin, *The Dispossessed*, Harper & Row, New York, 1974, pp. 288–9.

20   Keith Melville, *Communes in the Counter Culture: Origins, Theories, Styles of Life*, Morrow, New York, 1972, pp. 114–43.

21   Lewis Mumford, *The Pentagon of Power* as quoted on p. 58–59 in Judson Jerome, *Families of Eden: Communes and the New Anarchism*, Seabury Press, New York, 1974.

22   Rosabeth Moss Kanter, "Commitment and Social Organization: A Study of Commitment Mechanisms in Utopian Communities," *American Sociological Review*, vol. 33, no. 4, 1968, pp. 449–517.

23   Rosabeth Moss Kanter, *Commitment and Community: Communes and Utopias in Sociological Perspective*, Harvard University Press, Cambridge, Mass. 1972.

24   David Black, "Commune Children," *New Times*, vol. 6, no. 9, 30 April 1976, p. 34ff.

25   Jerome, *op. cit.*, p. 58.

26   P.B. Shelley, "A Defence of Poetry," in R.J. White, ed., *Political Tracts of Wordsworth, Coleridge and Shelley*, Cambridge University Press, 1953, p. 202.

27   Emma Goldman, *Anarchism*, 1910, as quoted in Paul Berman, ed., *Quotations from the Anarchists*, Praeger, New York, 1972, p. 28.

28   Jerome, *op. cit.*, p. 254.

29   *Ibid.*, p. 256.

30   Martin Duberman, *Black Mountain: An Exploration in Community*, Doubleday, New York, 1973. The individuals who participated in Black Mountain continue to relate to each other, to web vast numbers of persons in their life experiences. Though Black Mountain ceased to continue as a social order or community, its members have had a significant impact on the quality of life of humankind. The music, dance, art, weaving, poetry, litera-

ture, essays, technology, and philosophies of life of these persons have energized millions of persons and as well this book. Among those who participated in the Black Mountain experience were: Josef and Anni Albers, Eric Bentley, John Cage, Robert Creeley, Merce Cunningham, Buckminster Fuller, Paul Goodman, Charles Olson, Joel Oppenheimer, Arthur Penn, Charles Perrow, Robert Rauschenberg, Mary Caroline Richards, and many others.

31 Jerome, *op. cit.*, pp. 270–1.

32 *Ibid.*, p. 235.

33 Reinhard Bendix, "Sociology and the Distrust of Reason," *American Sociological Review*, October, 1970, vol. 35, no. 5, p. 834.

34 Shelley, *op. cit.*, p. 205.

35 *Ibid.*, pp. 205–6.

36 Bendix, *op. cit.*, p. 834.

37 Jerome, *op. cit.*, p. 236., Jerome is presenting ideas from Bookchin, *Post-Scarcity Anarchism, op. cit.*

38 E.F. Schumacher, *Small is Beautiful: A Study of Economics as if People Mattered*, Harper & Row, New York, 1973.

39 Jerome, *op. cit.*, p. 237.

40 Gerald Runkle, *Anarchism, Old and New*, Delacorte, New York, 1972, "Kropotkin's Evolutionary Ethics," pp. 58–62.

41 *Ibid.*, pp. 60–2.

42 Peter Kropotkin, *Ethics, Origin and Development*, Dial, New York, 1924, p. 97.

43 Runkle, op. cit., p. 135.

44 Michael Bakunin, "Principles and Organization of the Revolutionary Brotherhood," in Arthur Lehning, ed., *Michael Bakunin: Selected Writings*, Grove Press, New York, 1975. For a discussion of the concept of freedom see Aileen Kelley, "The Fatal Charm of the Millennium," *New York Review of Books*, 22 January 1976, and an exchange of letters between David T. Wieck and Aileen Kelley in *New York Review of Books*, 1 April 1976, p. 41.

45 Emma Goldman, "The Place of the Individual in Society," 1930s, as quoted in Berman, *op. cit.*, p. 162.

46 Emma Goldman, *Anarchism*, 1910, as quoted in Berman, *op. cit.*, p. 163.

47 Diane DiPrima, "Revolutionary Letter No. 47," *Revolutionary Letters, Etc.*, City Lights, San Francisco, 1971, p. 59.

Selected Readings

LAW: AN INSTRUMENT OF AUTHORITY

1 Albert R. Parsons, "Law versus Liberty," *Anarchism: Its Philosophy and Scientific Basis*, Mrs A.R. Parsons, Publisher, Chicago, Kraus Reprint Co., New York, 1971, pp. 186–7.
2 Daniel Berrigan, "A Question of Justice," *Catholic Worker*, vol. 42, no. 2, Feb. 1976, pp. 1, 3.
3 Peter Kropotkin, "Law and Authority," *Kropotkin's Revolutionary Pamphlets*, Benjamin Blom, N.Y., 1927, pp. 196–218.
4 John Griffiths, "Ideology in Criminal Procedure or A third 'Model' of the Criminal Process," *The Yale Law Journal*, vol. 79, no. 3, Jan. 1970, pp. 359–417.
5 Donald Black, *The Behaviour of Law*, Academic, New York, 1976.
6 David Miller, *Social Justice*, Clarendon, Oxford, 1976.
7 Peter Kropotkin, *Ethics: Origin and Development*, Dial, New York, 1924.
8 Harold E. Pepinsky, *Crime and Conflict*, Academic, New York, 1976.
9 Laura Nader, ed. *Law In Culture and Society*, Aldine, Chicago, 1969.
10 Laura Nader and Harry F. Todd, Jr, ed. *The Disputing Process – Law In Ten Societies*, Columbia University Press, New York, 1978.

SOCIAL HARMS: CRIME AND PENAL SANCTION

1 Peter Kropotkin, "Prisons And Their Moral Influence On Prisoners," *Kropotkin's Revolutionary Pamphlets*, Benjamin Blom, New York, 1927, pp. 220–35.
2 Hans Magnus Enzensberger, "Toward a Theory of Treason,"

and "Reflections Before a Glass Cage," pp. 1–19 and pp. 19–44 in *Politics and Crime*, translated Michael Roloff, Seabury Press, New York, 1974.

3   Paul Takagi, "The Walnut Street Jail: A Penal Reform to Centralize the Powers of the State," *Federal Probation*, Dec. 1975, vol. 39, no. 4, pp. 18–26.

4   Alexander Berkman, *Prison Memoirs of an Anarchist*, Schocken, New York, 1970.

5   *Crime and Social Justice, A Journal of Radical Criminology*, all volumes.

6   Richard Quinney, *Class, State, and Crime: On the Theory and Practice of Criminal Justice*, David McKay, New York, 1977.

7   Ian Taylor, Paul Walton, Jock Young, *The New Criminology: for a Social Theory of Deviance*, Routledge & Kegan Paul, London, 1973.

8   *Instead of Prisons: A Handbook for Abolitionists*, Prison Research Education Action Project, 3049 E. Genesee Street, Syracuse, New York, 13224, 1976.

9   Harold E. Pepinsky, *Crime and Conflict*, Academic, New York, 1976.

10 Harold E. Pepinsky, "Communist Anarchism As An Alternative To The Rule of Criminal Law," *Contemporary Crises*, 2 (1978) pp. 315–34.

11 Dennis C. Sullivan, *Corrections In America: The Mask Of Love*, Kennikat Press, Port Washington, N.Y., 1979.

12 Larry L. Tifft, "The Coming Redefinitions of Crime: An Anarchist Perspective," *Social Problems*, vol. 26, no. 4, April 1979, pp. 392–402.

13 Paul Goodman, *Growing Up Absurd*, Vintage, New York, 1956.

THE STATE

1   Peter Kropotkin, "The State: Its Historic Role," pp. 1–43 in Waldo R. Browne, *Man Or The State?*, Huebsch, New York, 1919.

2   Colin Ward, "Anarchy and The State," pp. 17–27 in *Anarchy in Action*, Harper, New York, 1974.

3   Leo Tolstoy, "Esarhaddon, King of Assyria," pp. 74–80 in *Fables And Fairy Tales*, translated Ann Dunninan, New American Library, New York, 1962.

4   David A. Gold, Clarence Y.H. Lo, and Erik Ohlin Wright,

"Recent Developments in Marxist Theories of the Capitalist State," *Monthly Review*, Oct. 1975, pp. 29–43 and Nov. 1975, pp. 36–51.

5 Noam Chomsky, *American Power and the New Mandarins*, Pantheon, New York, 1969.
6 Robert Nozick, *Anarchy, State & Utopia*, Basic, New York, 1974.
7 Franz Oppenheimer, *The State*, trans. John Gitterman, Free Life, 1975.
8 Tom Nairn, "The Twilight of the British State," *New Left Review*, nos. 101–2, Feb.–April 1977, pp. 3–61.
9 Michael Taylor, *Anarchy and Cooperation*, Wiley, London, 1976.
10 Hryhori Nestor Rudenko, *Anarchy*, unpublished manuscript.
11 Tifft and Sullivan, "Anarchy: A Non-Sequitor of Criminology, A New Vision of Justice and Social Order Without the State", paper presented at the American Society of Criminology meetings, Atlanta, Georgia, 1977.

THE WISH TO BE FREE: COMMITMENT TO EDEN

1 Murray Bookchin, *Post-Scarcity Anarchism*, Ramparts Press, San Francisco, 1971, esp. pp. 33–54 and 85–139.
2 Colin Ward, "The Organization of Anarchy," pp. 386–96 in Leonard I. Krimerman and Lewis Perry, eds., *Patterns of Anarchy*, Doubleday, New York, 1966.
3 Leo Tolstoy, "The Three Questions," *Fables and Fairy Tales*, translated Ann Dunnigan, New American Library, New York, pp. 82–8.
4 Ursula K. Le Guin, *The Dispossessed*, Harper & Row, New York, 1974.
5 Tifft and Sullivan, "From Possessed Sociology to Anarchism: A Journey and Return from Exile," pp. 180–97 in Joseph W. DeBolt, editor, *Ursula K. Le Guin: Voyager To Inner Lands and Outer Space*, Kennikat Press, Port Washington, N. Y., 1979.
6 Sam Dolgoff, *The Anarchist Collectives: Workers' Self-management in the Spanish Revolution 1936–1939*, Free Life, New York, 1974.
7 Ivan Illich, *Tools for Conviviality*, Harper & Row, New York, 1973.
8 Ivan Illich, *Toward A History of Needs*, Pantheon, New York, 1977–8.
9 Martin Duberman, *Black Mountain*, Dutton, New York, 1972.
10 Peter Kropotkin, *Ethics: Origin and Development*, Dial, New

York, 1924.
11 Christie & Meltzer, *The Floodgates of Anarchy*, Kahn & Averill, London, 1979.

Publishers:

Black Rose Books, 3934 St. Urbain, Montreal, Quebec.
Freedom Press, Angel Alley, 84B Whitechapel High Street, London E.1.
Free Life Editions, 41 Union Square West, New York, N.Y. 10003.
Cienfuegos Press, Over The Water, Sanday, Orkney Islands, KW17 2BL, Scotland.
Black Thorn Books, 186 Willow Avenue, Somerville, Mass. 02144, USA
Jura Press, 417 King St., Newtown, Sydney, Australia

Journals and Newspapers:

Anarchy, 37a Grosvenor Avenue, London, N5
Our Generation, Black Rose Books
Black Rose, Box 474 Somerville, Mass. 02144
Black Flag/Cienfuegos Press Anarchist Review, Orkney
Freedom, Freedom Press
Open Road, Box 6135 Station G., Vancouver, B.C. Canada
Soil of Liberty, Box 7056, Powderhorn Station, Minneapolis, Minn. 55407
Black Star, Mil-SRAF, Box 92 246, Milwaukee, Wisc. 53202.
SRAF Bulletin, SRAFprint, Box 4091, Mountain View, California 94040
Against The Grain, Box 692, Old Chelsea Station, New York, N.Y. 10011
Freespace Newsletter, 339 Lafayette, New York, N.Y. 10012
Fifth Estate, 4403 Second Avenue, Detroit, Mich. 48201

Bibliographical Notes:

Nicholas Walter, "Anarchism in Print: Yesterday and Today;" pp. 147–68 in David E. Apter and James Joll, *Anarchism Today*, Doubleday, New York, 1972.
Robert Goehlert, "Anarchism: A Bibliography of Articles 1900–1975," *Political Theory*, Feb. 1976, pp. 113–27.